After six years in a Thai refugee camp and a twenty-five hour flight from Bangkok, the Mom family arrives at Logan Airport. A few hours later they began their new life in Lowell.

From *Southeast Asians: A New Beginning in Lowell* (1985)

The Big Move

Immigrant Voices from a Mill City

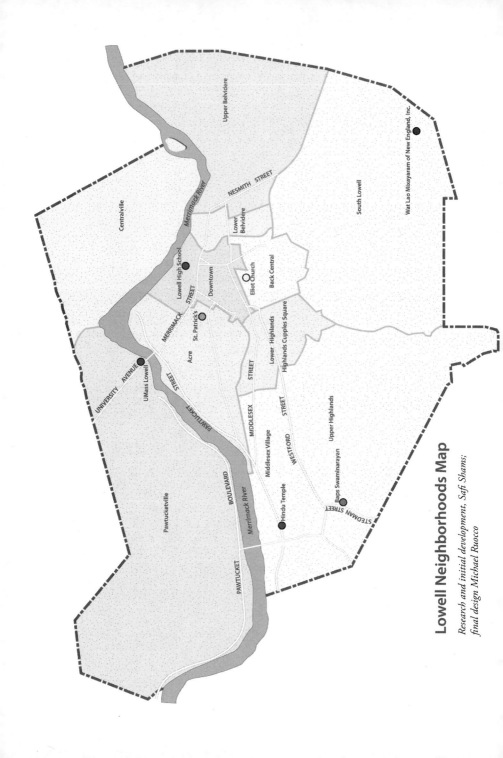

Lowell Neighborhoods Map

*Research and initial development, Safi Shams;
final design Michael Ruocco*

The Big Move

Immigrant Voices from a Mill City

Robert Forrant
and
Christoph Strobel

Loom Press
LOWELL, MASSACHUSETTS
2011

Printed in the United States of America
First Edition

Design: Higgins & Ross / higginsross.com
Photographs: James Higgins
Cover art: Anabelle Cristina Souza and Atena Vilorio Hernandez
Typeface: Adobe Garamond Pro
Printing: Thomson-Shore, Inc.

www.loompress.com
www.facebook.com/loompress
info@loompress.com

SPECIAL THANKS
Revolving Museum: Through public art, exhibitions, and educational
programs, the Revolving Museum of Lowell, Mass., promotes artistic
exploration and appreciation. The Revolving Museum encourages
community participation and growth, and provide opportunities for
individual empowerment and collective change.
www.revolvingmuseum.org

Mural Crew: The Revolving Museum Mural Crew transforms public
space. Students learn how to create blueprints and the rules of scaling,
interpret drawing and design, and create on a grand scale.

Immigrant Mural Project Funding: The mural project that produced
the cover art was supported with a grant from the University of
Massachusetts President's Office Creative Economy Initiative.

National Park Service Ethnography Project N1780060011:
Superintendent Michael Creasey and David Blackburn, Chief of Cultural
Resources and Programs at the Lowell National Historical Park, for their
support of the project, which focused on the history of ethnicity and
immigration in the Lowell area from the period of the first contact with
Native Americans to the present.

Contents

To our families and the immigrants and natives who continue making history in Lowell, Massachusetts

Acknowledgements

This book is a spin-off from a larger project completed for the National Park Service in December 2010, and we extend our thanks to them for funding Ethnography Project N1780060011. Special thanks to Superintendent Michael Creasey and David Blackburn, Chief of Cultural Resources and Programs at the Lowell National Historical Park, for their support of the project, which focused on the history of ethnicity and immigration in the Lowell area from the period of the first contact with Native Americans to the present. As part of that effort we collected a corpus of 35 oral histories with newcomers to the city of Lowell. We thank everyone who shared their stories with us. Several of these interviews appear in this volume, and our deepest gratitude is extended to those interviewees who graciously agreed to have their stories made even more public.

We are indebted to several of our colleagues and students. In particular, Linda Silka and Susan Thompson were valuable members of our research team, until in both cases changes in their careers necessitated their leaving the project; ours was the loss. Craig Thomas and Yingchan Zhang, 2008 M.A. graduates of the University of Massachusetts Lowell's Department of Regional Economic and Social Development, contributed greatly to the National Park report and assisted us with several of the interviews. Scott Walfield, Kim Scarfo, and Andrew Pearson, three University of Massachusetts Lowell history majors, also contributed to the report. We want to extend our appreciation to Nancy Hodge, Cheryl Rayner, and Janine Whitcomb for their hard work transcribing the oral histories.

A special thanks to Paul Marion and Loom Press for believing in the value of the individual stories that appear in this book. And, to Anabelle Cristina Souza and Atena Vilorio Hernandez, who produced the book's cover art, your creativity vividly conveys the stories inside of this book—thank you so much.

CHAPTER ONE

"The New Lowellians":
An Introduction to the History of Global Immigrants in an "All-America City"

Background

In the nineteenth century the global industrial revolution and immigration left their marks on the Merrimack Valley in general and Lowell in particular. The emergence of manufactories, mills, and canals slowly transformed the landscape where the Concord and the Merrimack Rivers joined. Early on industrial producers recruited Yankee women to work in their textile mills, but by the 1830s and with a rush in the 1840s there was a growing presence of immigrants from Ireland and other parts of Europe making their homes in the region. Immigrant workers—male and female—soon replaced the daughters of Yankee yeomen farmers in many of Lowell's mills carrying with them their many languages, rich customs, deep religious traditions, and sturdy backs bent to hard labor. In *Repositioning North American Migration History* Marc Rodriguez offers this point.

> Human history is a history of migration. Migration has long connected North America to the wider world and organized the continent into separate peoples, regions, and eventually individual nation states. Throughout American history, people have moved around within the boundaries of the United States and across the lines that have separated it from Canada, Mexico, the Caribbean, Europe, and Asia.[1]

What took place in and around Lowell, Massachusetts, since the early 1800s affirms Rodriguez's observation. Central to Lowell's story is this ever-changing workforce through the periodic rise and fall of mill employment through the 1920s followed by the city's rebirth as a high technology showcase, the home to the Lowell National Historical Park and its attendant historical preservation, numerous public-private partnerships building on the city's wonderful "old bones," and more recently as a city intent on playing a leading role in cultural production. Through these various transformations newcomers have been in the middle of the action, starting businesses, restoring old neighborhoods through their sweat equity, and contributing in numerous ways to the sorts of cultural activities that make Lowell an exciting place to be. No one can deny that the city's culinary scene, its music, its art, and its civic spirit have been energized by the thousands of immigrants who've made it their home over the last thirty or so years.

Frederick Coburn, in his multi-volume *History of Lowell and Its People* observes that the city "has yielded to no fell clutch of circumstances." When the labor supply from New England's rural towns was exhausted, employers sent recruiters to Quebec, Greece, Poland and numerous stops in between for workers. "Adventurous folks from other lands," Coburn writes, "seeking the advantages of a political democracy, are welcomed as workers. A few members of a nationality establish themselves, and these are quickly followed by others from the same foreign town or countryside." Paul McGouldrick writes that from the 1840s through approximately the 1880s, the daughters of Yankee yeomen farmers were replaced in the mills by "male and female workers of immigrant origin, who remained the almost exclusive source of labor supply until the 1920s."[2]

Immigrants remained the major source of labor until the 1920s when Congressional legislation dramatically slowed the entry of new immigrants to the United States with the passage of the Immigration Act of 1924. The law imposed a quota system, which made it particularly hard for immigrants from eastern and southern Europe (as well as the non-western world) to enter the United States.

Lowell's recent immigration history is part of national developments spurred on with the passage of the Immigration and Nationality Act of 1965. Since then, the United States received the most diverse group of immigrants in its history. The act eliminated the national origin quotas established in 1924, during a period of U.S. history characterized by significant anti-immigration activities. The quotas were based on the national origins of immigrants included in the 1890 census before the significant influx of immigrants from eastern and southern Europe occurred in the 1890s and early twentieth century. The 1924 Act also curtailed Asian immigration to the United States.

The passage of the 1965 Act opened the U.S. to immigrants from Asia, Latin America, the Middle East, and Africa. Hence, and unlike in the nineteenth and early twentieth century, when the majority of immigrants to the United States came from Europe, the latest wave of newcomers arrived from the non-western world. Among the new immigrants there is a tremendous diversity in terms of race, culture, language, religion, class, economics, connections to the homeland, and politics. In their daily life, the newcomers are preserving, creating, and re-inventing their traditions, ways of life, customs, and practices.[3]

Since the 1970s, thousands of immigrants have moved into Lowell, a city of about 104,000 people situated in the Merrimack River Valley in the northeastern part of Massachusetts. According to the U.S. Census Bureau, 22.1 percent of Lowell's population in the year 2000 was foreign born.[4] Just as the presence of foreign-born newcomers in the nineteenth and early twentieth centuries reshaped Lowell's religious practices, neighborhood character, foodways, and spoken languages, this latest wave of arrivals is changing the face of the city once again. Like earlier generations, new immigrants are shaping and enriching Lowell with their unique and diverse presence as they make the city their home. They own and operate hundreds of businesses, are a significant part of the labor force, and are active participants in and creators of cultural, social, as well as community organizations and institutions.

The latest wave of immigrants has significantly impacted Lowell; after suffering population losses for several decades, its population rose from 92,418 in 1980 to about 104,000 in 2010. This increase moves counter to the state's overall population loss. Between 2000 and 2005, for example, Massachusetts had a net loss of 230,000 inhabitants. This decline was accompanied by a net loss of jobs and a somewhat contradictory jump in house and condominium prices until the real estate market crisis starting in late 2006. The state's population loss was somewhat offset by the inflow of 160,000 immigrants, many of whom took low wage jobs in the service, health care, and the ever shrinking manufacturing sector. Employment in health care and the service sector—though smaller in numbers than late nineteenth century mill employment—served as an entryway into the labor market for many new Lowellians. However, it would be naïve to see immigrants only at the lower end of the economic spectrum. They also fill many high paying jobs in the Commonwealth's high tech and biomedical fields requiring highly skilled and educated labor.[5]

Who Is Here?

As the twenty-first century opened Lowell truly was a global city, much as it had been at the start of the twentieth century. Many of its foreign born and second-generation residents hailed from Southeast Asia, Latin America, Africa, and India. Cambodians, Vietnamese, and Lao constitute a significant portion of the population. In 2000, according to estimates by the Massachusetts Office for Refugees and Immigrants (MORI), 17,371 Southeast Asians lived in Lowell. Unofficial estimates put the number of Southeast Asians at 20,000 to 25,000. Southeast Asians make up about a quarter to a fifth of the city's overall population. About ninety percent of Southeast Asians in Lowell are believed to be Cambodian, about four to five percent Vietnamese, and another four to five percent Laotian. There is also a small community of Burmese in the city.[6]

The 2000 U.S. Census suggests that nearly 15,000 Latinos live in Lowell, though informal estimates come closer to 19,000 to 20,000. Census numbers indicate that nearly eight thousand Portuguese speakers live in the city, though unofficial estimates nearly double this number. Due to the issue of undocumented immigration, it is virtually impossible to get an accurate count of Portuguese and Spanish speakers in Lowell. Three to 4,000 Indians reside in Lowell, coming mainly from the state of Gujarat in western India as well as from the southern portion of the subcontinent. Many Indians live in Middlesex Village, the Highlands, and across the Merrimack, off Pawtucket Boulevard, a major street along the north side of the river that is dotted with numerous housing developments. Several Indian stores, restaurants, and two Swaminarayan temples are in Middlesex Village. There is also a growing cultural mosaic in the city of approximately 6,000 Africans. Sending countries including Cameroon, Liberia, Sierra Leone, Kenya, and Ghana.

Migration Stories

There are many reasons why immigrants came to the U.S. and ended up in Lowell. Some fled and continue to flee war, genocide, and repression. Others were and are looking for improved opportunities and a better life. This section provides a glimpse at the migration stories of some of Lowell's main immigrant groups, but it is by no means a complete account.

Most refugees from Cambodia left their country as a result of the Khmer Rouge's actions. This regime, which ruled Cambodia from 1975-1979, ordered the evacuation of cities, forcing people, including the sick and elderly, to move to the countryside with virtually no opportunity to prepare. In its efforts to create a "classless" society, the Khmer Rouge abolished the use of money, markets, banks, and private property. Schools closed, Buddhists nuns and monks were persecuted and Buddhist temples were desecrated. Intellectuals, political and religious leaders, artists, those who resisted, and even many of its own supporters who were suspected or alleged to be traitors were targeted. Forced into horrendous labor conditions, often without adequate food supplies, people died from starvation, sheer exhaustion, and the brutal torture and targeted murder that occurred in the "killing fields."

The Khmer Rouge period brought a reign of terror and horror to Cambodia. An estimated two million people (out of a population of less than eight million) died. The 1978 invasion of Cambodia by Vietnamese forces, and the installment by the Vietnamese of a new government in the country forced the Khmer Rouge into retreat. Vietnam's military interference also led 600,000 Cambodians to flee to Thailand and other surrounding countries where they were settled in refugee camps. Many were eventually relocated to new host societies that agreed to take them in.

In Vietnam, the pull out by U.S. forces in 1975 led to a flood of refugees. Many of those who attempted to escape had supported the United States' occupation and anti-communist struggle in the country. The boat people, as this group of refugees is often called because many fled by boat, underwent a harrowing experience. "It was a very dangerous journey," told Tony Mai. We were in "a little wooden boat about thirty feet long and it carried about seventy people exactly." The refugees feared that bad weather might sink their small vessels. They dreaded potential pirate attacks, which could mean theft, rape, murder, and other dangers. Yet despite these challenges, many Vietnamese refugees felt that there was no option but to leave.[7]

Between 1975 and 1992, some 220,000 people from Laos came to the United States as refugees. The Laotians are of a variety of different ethnic backgrounds belonging to the Hmong and various groups of the lowland Lao. Many in the first wave of refugees entering the United States in the early 1980s came as a result of a civil war that took place in the country. In many instances, the Laotian refugees had been allies of the Americans and had either participated themselves or were family members of people who had had participated in the conflict that became known in the United States as the "secret war" against the communist Pathet Lao. Later groups of Laotians left their country because they experienced hardship under the new government, they wanted to reunite with family members, or they sought more economic and educational opportunities.[8]

The U.S. government, as a matter of policy, attempts to disperse refugee populations. This is in part done to not overburden local government budgets, and to encourage the "assimilation" of refugees into American culture. However, refugees often pursue different goals. Once in the United States, various factors can lead them to move to certain locations that have a growing community of their peers. Historian Sucheng Chan argues that Lowell possessed three important elements that attracted Cambodians in the 1980s. First, she maintains, Kitty Dukakis, the wife of then Massachusetts Governor Michael Dukakis, was committed to providing assistance to the victims of the Cambodian genocide. Involved in local initiatives, she traveled to Thailand and lobbied on Cambodian refugee issues. The state government organized support agencies and provided public assistance programs. Second, during part of the 1980s, greater Lowell employers created many low-skill manufacturing jobs in the computer business—a period since then referred to as the "Wang boom." This period of economic growth ended, yet during the boom times assembly plants readily hired Cambodians looking for work. The third factor attracting Cambodian refugees to Lowell was the existence of a temple led by a well-known monk from Cambodia, located in nearby North Chelmsford.[9] Oral histories also suggest that Southeast Asians were attracted to Lowell to join family already in the city and to live within a large and lively community with ethnic food stores and businesses and relatively affordable housing.[10]

While one should not over-generalize the complex and diverse experiences and motivations of Latino immigrants, many were lured to the Lowell area by a desire to find jobs and to improve their economic opportunities. It is hard to find a distinct pattern in Latino migration stories. One exception may be the Colombians. The textile industry brought this particular group to the city in the 1960s and 1970s. The Colombians were thus another group of textile laborers, preceded by the Irish, Greeks, French Canadians, and many others. While Lowell saw a significant decline in the textile industry after the Second World War, with many companies leaving the Merrimack River Valley, a few companies remained. Wannalancit Mills, Ames Textile Corporation, and Joan Fabrics Corporation, among others, stayed in business for some time into the second half of the twentieth century.

Many of the Colombians who came to Lowell were skilled laborers who had worked in the textile industry in the Medellin area. Lowell's mills were in need of workers, because by U.S. standards, working conditions were undesirable, wages low, and benefits scarce, and there was little job stability.[11] Over the decades, however, the pattern of Colombian immigration changed. According to one interviewee, the recent influx of immigrants consists of "engineers" and "all kinds of educated people… Most of them speak English, and they want to do an MA, they want to study, they want to do many things, but it's not like before. There are still people who come to work. But not like before."[12]

The Gujarati from India have long participated in global migrations, going at least back to their involvement in the Indian Ocean trade, a trade system that reached from eastern Africa to China and peaked from the 800s to 1750.[13] During this period, Gujarat produced much of the cloth that dressed the Indian Ocean World. In the early 1900s, as a result of British imperialism, the Gujarati assumed a strong presence in eastern Africa as traders, especially in Tanzania and Uganda. There, they maintained frequent contacts with India and preserved a distinct Gujarati culture and identity, and prospered economically (often to the envy of the local African populations). Links with the homeland remained strong. Gujarati in the diaspora, for example, frequently sent their children and relatives to Gujarat, while in turn, receiving family members and close kin from India.

During the 1960s national liberation struggles in Africa the Gujarati were openly associated with the former European colonial masters by some anti-colonial activists, and faced discrimination and sometimes violence. Many Gujarati left the region for India, the United Kingdom, and the United States. The Gujarati in Lowell maintain frequent contact with relatives in India via telephone, e-mail, and through visits. They also interact with relatives in European countries, especially the United Kingdom, and with members of the extensive Gujarati communities spread all over the United States in states like New Jersey, California, and Texas.[14]

The migration stories and backgrounds of the Africans in Lowell are as diverse and varied as the continent from which they came. Many Africans come in search for better economic opportunities and were able to win a "green card" in the immigration lottery, which grants them a permanent home in the United States. Some came here to connect or re-connect with family members or to seek an education. Others fled political crisis in their sending societies such as repressive regimes or civil wars. In numerous instances a combination of economic and political factors spurred Africans to immigrate to the United States.

Africans live in several Lowell neighborhoods. There is certainly a center of African immigrant activity in Centralville where several African shops and an African church are located. Many Africans live in this neighborhood to the north of the Merrimack River as well as in adjacent Pawtucketville. There are also several African churches and businesses south of the river. Furthermore, many African immigrants rent and own apartments and houses south of the river.

Enterprise and Consumers

The wealth of immigrant businesses and restaurants in Lowell has become a vital and vibrant component of the city's economy. They serve immigrant customers and they are also frequented by mainstream consumers and by immigrants from different ethnic backgrounds. A number of Cambodian businesses are located around Pailin and Cupples Square in the Highlands and are sprinkled throughout other sections of this neighborhood and all over the city. Cambodian community leader Samkhann Khoeun describes this entrepreneurial activity:

> I think there is one furniture business owned by Cambodian-
> Americans and there are a few liquor stores… Then of course
> restaurants, insurance agencies, things of that nature. Then I think
> there's one or two driving schools, but again it's small scale as well.
> Hmm, you know, Laundromats. There's one on Westford and
> Chelmsford, and then motor shops and mechanics, you know…
> Businesses tend to grow in the area where there is a need in the
> community. They really tailor to the non-English-speaking
> clientele. So a lot of folks just take their car to have a new engine
> put in at a Cambodian-American body shop. And jewelry, there's
> many jewelry shops too.[15]

While there are some large markets like the Battambang Market on Merrimack Street, generally businesses remain small. According to Khoeun, there are economic and cultural factors that explain why Cambodian businesses tend stay this way.

> [I]t's a cross-cultural component and the way businesses run and
> operate, all that kind of stuff is somewhat different. You know, the

Cambodian community lends each other free food and money to start out. We do a lot of things on a personal basis. We do not like to really sign contracts. So there is still that element happening in the Cambodian community here. In their mind they know what to do, you know. So there are still elements of cultural difference and to some extent, I don't think, the Cambodian-American community, the business community, really puts into good use the existing infrastructure in Lowell.[16]

Similar issues apply to other immigrant communities. Furthermore, Cambodian businesses, like immigrant businesses and start-ups in general, have a high failure rate. Business survival depends on the hard work and the long workdays of the owners who quite often toil six or seven days a week, usually with the help of family members who often pitch in as free or underpaid laborers.[17]

Numerous Latino, Portuguese, Brazilian, Indian, and African businesses and restaurants can be found across the city. Many of them cater to ethnic consumers' needs and desires. However, they do not just satisfy a commercial niche within the community, they also provide employment. Furthermore, due to discrimination in the labor market, self-employment is an attractive, and often the only alternative for economic mobility for many immigrants.[18]

Immigrants in Lowell also shop and eat at mainstream businesses and restaurants. While the ethnic stores serve an important function in many of the city's newcomer communities, immigrants note that mainstream supermarkets increasingly cater to their tastes and needs, often at lower prices than small stores can offer. Thus, many immigrants go to the malls in Nashua, New Hampshire, and Burlington, Massachusetts, and they shop at major grocery stores and retailers such as Costco, Wal-Mart, and Target. Immigrants go to movies and consume various other forms of mainstream American entertainment. But, they also consume entertainment from home as evidenced by the fact that several ethnic businesses in Lowell— whether Southeast Asian, Latino, Indian, or African—rent and sell videos and music from home. Finally, while many immigrants frequent the ethnic restaurants catering to their particular tastes, they also eat at mainstream restaurants.[19]

Organizations and Associations

Social science researchers and social workers frequently point out that immigrant populations have unique needs, especially when compared to the mainstream. Many come to the United States speaking little English, experience culture shock, and are unfamiliar with American customs, the political system, and public services. To help tackle these issues, immigrants have established various organizations.

The Cambodian Mutual Assistance Association of Greater Lowell (CMAA), founded in 1984, serves the needs of the Cambodian population. The CMAA runs and has run a daycare center, youth programs, programs for the elderly and children with developmental disabilities, civic education programs, a program for families undergoing intergenerational conflict, and a program for young parents. It has also sponsored programs to reintroduce Cambodians in Lowell to agriculture through the use of local farmlands, and a pilot project in fish farming.

The Massachusetts Alliance of Portuguese Speakers (MAPS) serves the Portuguese and Brazilian communities. With offices in Cambridge, Somerville, and Boston, the group expanded into Lowell in 1998. Located in Back Central, the neighborhood where many Portuguese speakers live, MAPS offers health and social services programs, ranging from domestic abuse assistance, to reading or translating correspondence, to calling a doctor for a prescription or an appointment.[20]

The African Assistance Center serves the needs of African immigrants and refugees in the city. It was founded in 2000. The AAC runs assistance programs focused on economic and immigration issues and it provides Africans with opportunities to socialize and to network.[21] Other cultural organizations cater to the needs of specific African groups in the city. The Cameroonians of Lowell Association (CAMOLA) are arguably the most active among these groups. CAMOLA lobbies politically for the interests of the Cameroonian community. The association does not only work to preserve Cameroonian culture but also attempts to showcase it to mainstream society. The organization celebrated its tenth anniversary in the summer of 2002 at an event at St. Anne's Church, attended by 600 people including several city officials and a Cameroonian notable and traditional ruler, King Agwafo III. The event featured Cameroonian food, music, crafts, and dance.[22]

Not all African national communities are as highly organized, but several groups have established networks assisting their communities and simultaneously engaging with the needs of their homeland. For example, on May 2, 2009, greater Lowell's Liberian community was instrumental in hosting the inaugural ball for the Massachusetts Alliance for the Restoration of the University of Liberia. The event raised badly needed funds for the institution, which had suffered during the civil war that devastated the country in the late 1990s and early 2000s.

Religious Life

Starting with the Irish, successive waves of immigrants enriched the city's religious landscape with their diverse belief systems, scriptures, customs, traditions and architecture. Quite often they've joined and strengthened existing church parishes and other religious institutions, and where necessary they've built new structures like Hindu and Buddhist temples, Christian churches, and places for Muslims to worship.

Buddhism is the major religion among Lowell's Southeast Asians and there are various temples in the area. For instance, a Lao Buddhist temple, named Watlao Mixayaram, is located in a quiet residential neighborhood in South Lowell just off Interstate 495. Here the monks reside in a building to the left of the main entrance to the small temple complex, much like the rectory arrangement found at many Catholic churches. On the right is the main temple hall, which was just built a few years ago. The main temple has a kitchen area in which women prepare food for the monks and at times for the community visiting the temple for festivals and holy days. As you enter the main hall of the temple you can see the statue of a golden Buddha sitting on an altar. The hall is encircled with paintings depicting aspects of Buddha's life story.

Churches play an important role in the lives of many immigrants. The congregation at the Elliot Church, for instance, is about one third Cambodian, one third African, and one third white. Moreover, a significant part of the Vietnamese population in Lowell is Catholic, and the Church of Latter Day Saints is a chosen place of worship among some Southeast Asians. St. Patrick's Church is a popular place for the Vietnamese of greater Lowell to socialize and network, usually on Saturday, the same day when mass is given in Vietnamese. The church's Vietnamese community has a youth group. Meetings are held to prepare for holidays like the Vietnamese New Year or to organize the group's ping-pong tournaments. Church membership or being a Christian is not a prerequisite to attend social evens, which are open to everyone regardless of their religious affiliation.[23]

Due to regional and sectarian variations in Hinduism, there is tremendous diversity among U.S. immigrants who identify as Hindu. Peter Occhiogrosso, a scholar of world religions, describes Hinduism as "an endlessly complex and varied collection of beliefs and belief systems, but they are all based on ideas and principles that can be traced back to an extensive collection of scriptures called the Veda."[24] Religious life centers on their temples for many in the Indian community. Hindu temples contain sacred images and statutes of Hindu deities, with services taking place several times a day in temples that are often left open during the day for attendees to worship.

Lowell's two Hindu temples are in industrial buildings on Stedman Street and Middlesex Street. Lowell's temples are Swaminarayan institutions, named after the founder of this sect of Hinduism, but a different line of gurus leads each. Predominantly attended by Gujaratis, they also attract Indians who originate from other regions in India. The membership and visitors to the temple tend to live in the Lowell area, but attendees travel from southern New Hampshire, and Waltham, Beverly and Worcester in Massachusetts. These worshipers are sometimes former residents of Lowell, but quite often they belong to a particular Swaminarayan and are willing to travel a long distance to worship and to meet with members of their faith community. Lowell's Indian residents also attend the Chinmaya Mission temple in Andover or the Sri Lakshmi temple in Ashland. Both temples in Lowell have gender segregation during worship, something not common to all Hindu temples. In the Steadman Street facility the men sit in front and women in the back. In the Swaminarayan temple on Middlesex Street men and women sit on opposite sides of the facility. The temples draw especially large crowds during festivals.

The temples actively raise money for charitable work such as disaster assistance, which can be nationally as well as internationally focused. For example, the temple on Steadman Street is an affiliate BAPS Care International, which conducts an annual Walk-a-thon in Lowell to raise funds for various causes such as Hurricane Katrina relief. The temple and BAPS Care International were actively involved with disaster assistance and fundraising during the earthquakes in India, Pakistan, and Afghanistan, and during the tsunami catastrophe. BAPS Care International also runs literacy, health care, and housing programs, which the temple membership supports through donations and volunteering.[25]

African immigration has led to a proliferation of African churches in greater Lowell. The International Christian Fellowship Ministries story provides a glimpse into the growth of such churches. A congregation of less than twenty members in the late 1990s, it had over one hundred members by 2003. The group established its first church by purchasing an old restaurant on 1426 Gorham Street. In 2007 an average of 200 members attended each service and church leaders searched for a new facility. There are Liberian and Kenyan churches in the Highlands, and a Ghanaian church in downtown Lowell. Africans also attend mainstream churches, such as the Eliot Presbyterian Church and St. Michael's Catholic Church in the Centralville neighborhood.[26]

On occasion, religion can be a source of conflict. At the Trairatanaram Temple and Parsonage in North Chelmsford conflicts between monks resulted in a court order to separate the two factions into the upstairs and the downstairs portions of the temple. The dispute antagonized some members of the Cambodian community. Some in the community have lost their faith in the monks and argue that they've lost all claims to morality because they are tainted by a desire for power or by corruption.[27]

Festivals and Cultural Preservation

As in the past, language and cultural preservation are central issues for many newcomers. Immigrant groups organize festivals that celebrate their sending societies' cultures and showcase them to the mainstream society. Numerous community organizations and groups run cultural programs, dance groups, and language instruction programs. One of the largest of these efforts is the Southeast Asian Water festival, which takes place every August on the Merrimack River to celebrate, preserve, and share Southeast Asian culture. The celebration attracts 60,000 to 100,000 people every year. Attendees are certainly from the Lowell area, but many Cambodians, Lao, and Vietnamese annually travel to Lowell from across the country for the festival, which takes place:

> to thank the spirit of the water, to pray for evil spirits to go away, and
> to honor the Dragon King who dwells in the water. The Water Festival
> is a time to be thankful for the rivers, lakes and ponds that villagers
> depend upon for their livelihood and economic development. [28]

One festival highlight is the dragon boat races, in which crews of eighteen to twenty-four rowers compete in traditional Southeast Asian boats over a stretch of 1000 meters on the Merrimack River. There is a wealth of traditional Southeast Asian dance and traditional musical performances. But the dancers at times also mix in U.S. cultural elements such as hip hop and break dancing to lighten the mood, while teenagers and young adults perform rap music, often in Southeast Asian languages such as Khmer. Beauty pageants are also popular role during the festival. Scores of vendors line the festival site selling a rich variety of Southeast Asian foods, crafts, and traditional clothing.[29]

For nearly thirty years a Puerto Rican Festival has honored the island's culture and heritage and attracted Puerto Ricans from all over New England. In the past, activities included the dance troupe Estrellas Tropicales (Tropical Stars), orchestras, parades, and beauty pageants.[30] The Vietnamese community has staged a large Vietnamese New Year celebration since the 1980s. This event is co-organized by the St. Patrick's Church group and the UMass Lowell Vietnamese Student Association. Thong Phamduy, interviewed in this book, is a lead organizer and co-initiator of the celebration, which takes place at UMass Lowell's Cumnock Hall. Since 2001, the African community has held the Greater Lowell African Festival, a celebration of African culture, music, food, dance, and traditional dress. Bands perform African music and African food is being served. "The festival is an opportunity for me to showcase my culture and to get my neighbors and my American friends to sample our food and music" observed one of the co-organizers of the festival to the *Lowell Sun*. The Puerto Rican Festival, the Vietnamese New Year Celebration, and the Greater Lowell African Festival are three examples of the many festivals and traditional holiday celebrations Lowell's immigrant communities organize annually.[31]

Several organizations are active in the area of cultural preservation. As our oral histories point out, several immigrant groups have created programs to teach the younger generation their sending society's language. The Angkor Dance Troupe, a nationally recognized dance ensemble, plays a crucial role "keeping Khmer traditions alive for future generations" by practicing, performing, and preserving Cambodian classical and folk dance. A central feature of its mission is the teaching of traditional dance to the younger generation. A non-profit cultural organization, Angkor's mission is to: preserve, develop and teach the traditions of Cambodian performing arts; promote an increased understanding and appreciation for Cambodian culture through educational programs and professional public performances; support the work of Cambodian dancers in the U.S. and Cambodia; and provide in-depth, high quality arts training and leadership development opportunities for inner-city youth.[32] While the Dance Troupe aims to maintain Cambodian culture, the dancers also actively participate in processes of cultural creation. By fusing Cambodian dance with American musical elements such as rap and hip hop—blending the "traditional" with the "modern" in some of their performances— they are reinventing dance and at the same time creating a unique Cambodian American culture.[33]

Programs run by the Massachusetts Association of Portuguese Speakers educate the next generation of Portuguese speakers. Elderly women, for instance, volunteer to teach young girls how to sew, crochet, and embroider, a skill that many Portuguese speakers take much pride in. Young girls are kept off the streets, elderly women are involved in the community, and an aspect of their culture is passed down from one generation to the next.[34] It is important to remember though, that these examples merely provide a glimpse into the strategies that immigrants in Lowell have devised as they work to hold onto and preserve important aspects of their sending societies' culture. At the same time many of these examples also demonstrate how cultural preservation activities result in the creation of unique new forms of expression.

Transnational Lives

Some immigrants live what scholars describe as "transnational lives," spending time in their daily lives in the United States while they also remain, to varying degrees, active participants in their countries of origin. They do so by regularly visiting their families, by investing back home, by sending remittances to family members, and by supporting humanitarian programs in the so-called 'old country'. Immigrants may also own property in their countries of origin.

Many Lowell immigrants maintain transnational family connections by communicating with, and by visiting their relatives. Several of our interviewees point out that they talk to relatives on the phone, often using international phone cards to keep costs low. The younger generation maintains contacts through e-mail and instant messaging. Frequent trips abroad keep individuals connected to their families and their countries of origin. Lowellians also receive family visitors from abroad, though in recent years travel visas have been difficult to obtain. This change is due to increased security concerns since September 11, 2001, and to the intensifying national political debate over "illegal immigration," which has led federal authorities to be more stringent about granting travel permission to visitors from developing nations, for fear that they might overstay their visas.

Immigrants sometimes participate in transnational politics. For instance, some Cambodians in Lowell are involved in their sending society's political affairs. While this is a minority of people, there is enough involvement for Cambodian political parties to have active party apparatuses in Lowell. All major parties—the Cambodian People's Party (CPP), the Royal Party, and the Sam Rainsy Party—actively seek support among Lowell's Cambodians. David Turcotte and Linda Silka write, "these party loyalties continue to loom large and infrequently have led to conflict that has negatively impacted community development within Lowell." They add, "party activists hold influence within the community and their distrust of each other often prevents collaboration on important community initiatives." Among the Lao as well homeland politics stir passions. Community members argue over which specific flag should represent the Lao, some supporting the use of the official flag, while a minority advocates for the use of the royal flag that was flown in the country before the Pathet Lao communists took over in the 1970s. "As a result," write Turcotte and Silka, "divisions have emerged within the Lao refugee community that are now preventing collaborating to address local needs and issues within Lowell."[35]

Childrearing and meeting a future partner can become transnational affairs as well. An immigrant from Ghana explained that her parents in her hometown in Ghana are raising her children. This is not an unusual occurrence in immigrant communities nor is it uncommon for children to move back and forth between the United States and their parents' place of birth.[36] Marriage partners are sometimes found in the sending society or in a Diaspora community from a different country.[37]

Politics

As the oral histories herein demonstrate, political representation is an important issue for immigrants. Despite the overall size of the city's immigrant population, their political representation remained limited in 2010. Hurdles stand in the way of voting. One of them is the city's reliance on an at-large voting system—there is no representation by smaller geographic neighborhoods—for the city council and school committee, which makes it hard for immigrants to get elected to office. While an immigrant leader may be well know in his or her community, this does yet not translate into electoral success across Lowell. There is a general disinterest concerning politics among some in the immigrant community, just as there is in the mainstream society. Furthermore, a limited knowledge of English, a lack of information on voting laws and campaign procedures, and a fear of civic participation because of past political repression in their sending societies inhibit many newcomers from voting. In some cases voting is restricted due to the lack of citizenship.

Naturalization can be a cumbersome and intimidating process. Various organizations in Lowell offer assistance with citizenship classes and organize voter registration drives. MAPS helps individuals fill out their citizenship applications and readies applicants for the process through various classes. Organizations like One Lowell run voter registration drives and voter education programs which create awareness about the importance of voting. Still the struggle for more adequate political representation will need to be continued in the future.[38]

Immigrant Voices

The United States is a nation of great diversity. Its people come from all corners of the globe carrying essential elements of their cultures with them. In deciding what they can and must bring, immigrants consciously choose to begin the complex process of preserving various aspects of their cultural identities as they adjust to a new place, new ways of making a living, a new culture, and a new civil society. These processes have occurred throughout Lowell's history and the nearly 400-year encounter between alien and established groups is a dramatic story indeed, one with its share of confrontation and accommodation. People with various backgrounds and religions adjusted to their new surroundings and it appears that more often than not a middle ground was found that bridged cultural differences. However, flashpoints and conflict occurred during periods of economic and political instability and fear.

Despite outside pressures, individuals and groups sought out ways to imagine and maintain their identity through the preservation, creation, and re-invention of traditions, ways of life, customs, and practices. The establishment of churches, foreign-language schools, and social clubs are manifestation of this process. Immigrant food markets and restaurants, barbershops, coffee house, and foreign-language newspapers helped to continually make and remake Lowell. The history of immigration in the All-America City is ongoing and this introduction has barely scratched the surface of its rich complexity.

To summarize, since the 1970s Lowell has attracted its fair share of newcomers. Just as the presence of immigrants in the nineteenth and early twentieth century altered and influenced the city, the latest wave of arrivals is literally changing the face of Lowell. Like earlier generations, these New Lowellians are enriching the city with their unique and diverse presence as they make it their new home. As their nineteenth century counterparts did, they've built new religious institutions or joined existing one, started hundreds of small businesses, many of them at the former sites of markets, bakeries, and restaurants owned by previous immigrants like the French-Canadians and the Greeks. They've contributed to the city's post-1980 renaissance by being active participants in and creators of vibrant cultural, social, and community organizations and institutions.

We are thankful to the nine individuals who've agreed to share their stories with you and us in this book. Untainted by the analytical eye of historians, sociologists, anthropologists, and political scientists we hope the words of these nine people provide an important glimpse into the lives led by Lowell' recent immigrants. Certainly the rich complexity of that experience is impossible to put forward in one book but we believe that much can be learned from the perspectives and voices herein and we are quite excited that these oral histories can be shared with a larger audience.

CHAPTER TWO

Phala Chea

Phala came to the U.S. with her family in 1981 as a refugee from Cambodia. Currently she works for the Lowell Public Schools as a Specialist for Community Outreach in Support of English Language Learners and Families. Prior to this position, she worked as the Coordinator of the Parent Information Center for seven years, an Equity Facilitator for one year, and a teacher for six years. She has served as the President of the Cambodian Mutual Assistance Association and as Treasurer of the Southeast Asian Water Festival. Christoph Strobel interviewed Phala on January 15, 2008.

Lowell is known historically as a city of immigrants. In order to help immigrants and refugees transition smoothly and successfully in our society, we need to understand the adaptation process and the different background experiences that newcomers bring with them to Lowell. Through my own experience as a newcomer, I learned that when a newcomer arrives with strong educational background and strong skills that are transferable in his/her new setting, he/she is able to adapt quicker. As we are learning, this is not the case for many newcomers. Most of them arrived here with trauma, with fear, uncertainty and limited skills making adjustments and adaptation an every-day struggle. As a community, we need to work together and help encourage each other to become successful citizens.

My name is Phala Chea. I live in Lowell. I came from Cambodia.

What were the decisions that motivated you and your family to move to the U.S.?
We had a very difficult situation in our country. The Khmer Rouge took over

Cambodia from 1975 to1979. Because of that, we were forced to escape to save ourselves. So basically, my immediate family and I left Cambodia in 1979 and fled to refugee camps in Thailand.

And then through the refugee process there, you were able to get to the United States?
Yes. It took us about a year and a half to leave the camps because we had to go through the refugee application process and find a sponsor. We were able to locate my mother cousin's in Oregon. It took us a year and a half to get to the U.S. with his sponsorship.

Was Lowell the first place your family came to? Or was it as with many Cambodians around here that your parents went to different cities before they came to Lowell?
We went to Portland, Oregon first because that was where my mother's cousin lived.

What spurred you to move to Lowell?
After living in Oregon for about five years we heard through friends about the large population of Cambodians living here in Lowell. We wanted to find more comfort within our own community and to be closer to our relatives living in Montreal, Canada. So that's why we moved to Lowell.

You arrived in the mid-1980s?
In 1987.

What was your first impression when you came to the United States? Did you have any preconceptions about the U.S.?
We really didn't have any. I mean my parents went to an ESL class for three months. They learned about the culture of the United States. But then we really didn't know exactly what to expect just from what we've heard from teachers and what we could see in books. Seeing the actual United States was rather different from our imagination. We were quite shocked when we first arrived. The weather, the environment, the people and everything else around us were startlingly different from our imagination.

Did you live in a city in Cambodia, like Phnom Penh?
We lived in Phnom Penh and then the Khmer Rouge forced us to go to Battambang's countryside to work the fields, but we had very little experience in that area. We really didn't know much about planting and harvesting rice.

What was your first impression when you came to the city? Did you feel at home in the Cambodian community?

We felt more comfortable here, than living in Portland. We only knew a few families in Portland, so not enough for us to be comfortable, to be able to speak the language, and practice our culture and traditions. But coming here, we were able to go to temples, markets, and different Cambodian agencies when we needed to.

Do you plan to spend the rest of your life in Lowell? Or are you maybe thinking about moving to a different part of the country, or maybe to the suburbs?

It's hard to say. My family and I are getting used to Lowell. We are getting used to the snow and the different New England seasons. I don't know. If we do decide to move, it would be somewhere where we could continue to be together. We don't want to separate. Right now we are happy in Lowell. We have our work and our schools here.

Do you feel part of a neighborhood? I live around Cupples Square in the Highlands neighborhood.. People often say it is a Cambodian neighborhood. Do you feel that this is the case? Or is it more a consideration that I live here but I go shopping in the Highlands and if I have to, I go up to Nashua, New Hampshire How important is neighborhood to you?

It doesn't really have any importance. I just want a place where I can be safe and comfortable. I do my shopping all around town. Sometimes when I'm hungry for Cambodian food, I would go to the restaurants around the area or the supermarkets to find different food.

Are there any specific businesses you go to for groceries? Do you go exclusively to Cambodian stores? Or do you also go to places like Market Basket or Hannaford's?

I shop everywhere for food. Sometimes when I'm busy, I shop within close range of my house. I can go to Market Basket downtown or the Asian markets nearby.

Have you traveled much outside of Lowell? Maybe up to Montreal to meet your family, back to Oregon, or back to Cambodia?

I've traveled quite a bit to Montreal, to California, and Texas where we have relatives. I haven't returned to Oregon yet. I hope to go there soon. I only returned once to Cambodia.

Where do most of your friends and family live? Do they reside all over the city?

All over the city, yes… My family lives in Belvidere, and I have a lot of friends in the Acre and a lot of friends in the Highlands as well.

When you are in the Highlands or in the Acre does that feel to you like a Cambodian neighborhood? Do you feel more comfortable in the Highlands than in Belvidere? Does it matter?
If I want to do activities or be involved in the same culture, then I would probably be more comfortable going to the Highlands or the Acre area where there are more Cambodian families.

How does your family stay together? You made the point that family is very important to you. Does most of your family at this point live in Lowell?
My parents and I live in Lowell. My brother and sister live in Boston.

Do you still have family in Cambodia?
Yes, cousins, aunts and uncles.

Do you communicate with folks in Cambodia a lot via e-mail or telephone?
Yes, phone and e-mails.

Does family from Cambodia ever come to visit you in the U.S.?
Only a few were able to get permission to come; others couldn't. They tried to come, but they couldn't get visas.

Is the admission process pretty strict?
Yes, very strict.

Is this from the Cambodian government's side or the U.S. government's side?
More on the U.S. side.

Do you feel your life is different from that of your parents? Do you feel more privileged than your parents have been?
I think so. They came here at a very tough age, middle age, and it was very hard for them to go to school because they had the responsibility of taking care of their children and be able to provide financially for the family. They had to support their children in education. So they've sacrificed a lot. And for me, because I had their support, I was able to do more with my life.

Do you consider Lowell your home?
Yes.

Do you feel that, the Cambodia language, the cultural heritage, still plays an important role in your life?
Very much so, I mean more so than when I was younger. When I was younger, the most important thing for me was to fit in at school and to fit in with my friends. I tried to assimilate and tried to be like them as best as I could. This meant even sacrificing my own language and my own culture at times. But I realized that my culture and language and my Khmer identity are very important, and that I should try to maintain it, and also work with the community to try to preserve it for the young generation as well.

Did you go to school both in Oregon and in Lowell?
Yes.

Did you feel that because there was a larger Cambodian community here that it was a little bit easier, or did that make it harder?
I attended elementary and middle schools in Portland, Oregon. When we first arrived I was enrolled in the fourth grade and then went on to middle school. We had very little. There were only maybe two or three other students with the same background as myself. I found that to be very difficult because I had really no one to communicate or relate with because they were in other classrooms. I didn't know the language when I first arrived. It was very difficult for me to understand what was happening in the classroom, what was happening at school. In Lowell you may have a teacher or sometimes a paraprofessional, or other students who you may talk to in your language.

So here there was more of a support network?
Yes.

You still speak Khmer?
Yes.

Do you feel like having those two languages is actually an asset or does that hold you back at times?
It's quite an asset in my line of work because I deal with a lot of families, many of whom are Cambodians. I work in a center where families come to register their

children for school and where they can learn about the school system. Or if they need help with anything, I'm able to communicate and assist them.

Again, and maybe to draw a comparison with your parents, how was language a different issue for them? Was it easy for them to learn English? Was that something that they always struggled with?

More so for my mother than my father. Both of them came here knowing French. They were somewhat able to relate and transfer some of that knowledge into English. My parents never had the opportunity to take in-depth ESL courses here. They really didn't have time to focus on learning English. So for them, they basically learned English in their work settings. Even now, my mother is not as proficient in English as she hopes to be. She just knows enough to get by. But for my father, he was able to continue his education in the U.S. and he is proficient in English.

Does your mother… it sounds like she works as well?
Yes.

Do you feel that it held her back professionally to not have the language ability? And that language and knowing English opened up doors to you and your father, opened up opportunities that she couldn't get?
Yes, I believe so. My mother's priority was to make sure that we succeed in school. She did not have the time to go to school to improve her English. This held her back.

Was it easier for her once you moved to Lowell because there was more of a community and more stores?
It was easier for her because she was able to speak Khmer with friends and community members.

Do you still support, either you or your family, relatives back in your homeland?
Yes, yes, we do.

Just immediate family or extended?
Extended.

Do you also make donations to schools or social institutions?
We do that as well; we donate. My parents actually are in Cambodia right now. For my mother it's her first time back; for my father, I think this is his third or fourth

time back. They are basically there to unite with their family members and to also help some of the villagers dig wells. Before they went, they were able to fund-raise some money for their well digging project.

Do you like the job that you are doing right now? Do you feel that you are making a difference? Sounds like you are the perfect person for the job.
I do. I like this job very much because I get to work with everyone living in Lowell. And then I get to work with different community members; I get to see newcomers come to Lowell.

Obviously you deal with a lot of Southeast Asians, but do you deal with other new immigrants as well?
We are beginning to see families from countries in Africa and Brazil. And we are still seeing, a few here and there from Vietnam and Cambodia.

And also a few Indians too?
A few.

If you could have any job that you wanted, what would that be?
It would be something similar to this one, where I can work with the community. Something in a social service field where I can help people to improve their lives.

Do you or your family attend religious services? Do you go to temple?
We do. Not as often as we would like to because of our work schedule. But we try to attend special ceremonies.

Theravada Buddhists?
Uh huh.

Which temple do you usually go to if you don't mind if I ask?
Well, there are three temples. One in Lowell here and then two – Upstairs and Downstairs in Chelmsford – we attend all three.

So there's not a specific one. Is that common?
It is fairly common. For us, we find that we get along with all three. And a lot of our friends go to all three. We go there with them. It doesn't really matter. I think for some people maybe they like one better than the other, but for me, I have no preference.

In the Jewish or Christian tradition you have one main day for worship? That's not the case with Buddhism, right? But do you feel that a lot of the worship activities are pushed to the weekends to accommodate people's working lives?

More so. Buddhism is everyday practice. It's part of our life. But for special occasions, special ceremonies, they are held back to the weekends to accommodate workers and students.

Are the Upstairs and Downstairs Temple able to resolve their issues?

I thought they were moving to resolve things. I think they are getting a little bit friendlier. I've always felt comfortable going to either one. I don't know how far they've gotten with the resolution.

Are there contacts between, and you might not know about this, the temples here and temples back in Cambodia? Are there interactions and exchanges?

Right. I know there are some, but I'm not sure to what extent exactly.

What do you do for fun? Do you go on vacations?

We do go on vacations. When we do, we mainly go up to Canada to spend time with our relatives or go to other states to visit our other relatives. Those are vacations. But if we want to do something locally, we'd probably go to visit our friends' homes around town or join them on special occasions at one of the local restaurants.

You said that you had relatives from Cambodia who came to visit. When they get permission to travel, if they get permission to travel, how long do they usually stay and when they are here, what do you do with them?

One time we had relatives staying for about six months. We showed them around Lowell and around the state and took them to New York and to California. We tried to show them as much as possible, because they usually don't get another chance to come here.

Wow! Did you take them to some of the Park museums as well?

We did. The National Park, the different mills and museums we have around here. We also took them to Boarding House Park to enjoy some of the music series we had. They even went to the folk festivals.

That's great! Do you have mostly Cambodian friends or do you have a wider network of friends?

I would say wider because I work with both groups–the mainstream as well as Cambodians.

Do you find that this is typical for most Cambodians? Does it matter if it's a person of the first generation or the second generation? In other words, does the same hold true for your parents? Or maybe is it the case for your father but not for your mother? So that language is an issue there?

Language is a major issue in determining which group you feel comfortable with. If you feel comfortable staying within your own community, then you do so. But for me, I try to make an effort to fit in mainstream society, so that I may be more successful in my work.

What are your favored types of celebrations or Buddhist religious festivals? Do you celebrate holidays like Christmas?

I celebrate everything, because celebration is celebration. You don't need to only practice your own religion or tradition. You do things that make you happy. Celebrate Christmas? Sure, that makes my family happy. We celebrate Thanksgiving as well because we value the opportunity to spend time with our family.

What are some of your favorite Buddhist holidays? Do you like the New Year Celebration?

For the New Year in April, we usually go to the temple in the morning and then go to a community celebration with our friends in the evening. We also have a big religious holiday in early fall where we honor and remember the lives of our loved ones who have died. So that's the time where we revere and memorialize the past and pray for peace and serenity. And that's a special time for us.

Are there activities at the temple or do you also celebrate that at home?

We often prepare food as an offering at home or take food to the temple.

Are you, a member of a neighborhood or a Cambodian cultural organization or anything of that sort?

I'm actually the president of the Cambodian Mutual Assistance Association (CMAA) and also a board member of the Southeast Asian Water Festival.

What are some of your responsibilities, and what challenges do you face?
Networking is a big task for me, and making connections with members of the community. As president, I want CMAA to be recognized by the mainstream community and I want to find ways to get more funding for the organization. These are my goals as well as my challenges. Each year, I feel that we have to scramble for city, state, and federal funding to keep our programs running. We try to do what we can to make our organization known to the public. We try to reach out to the community.

Do you find that the mainstream community is receptive to the work that the CMAA is doing or the Water Festival is doing? Is it up and down or do you feel that maybe now it's more supported than it was in the past?
I think we are getting more involvement from the city. I think they are starting to be more supportive, more so than in the past. The City Manager met with us several times to listen to our concerns and our issues. We are beginning to work closely with the Police Department as well. The Chief of Police is very nice. He is very open and very supportive of CMAA and is appreciative of our collaborative efforts. CMAA and other Southeast Asian organizations do not want to work in isolation— we want to work with the city to help improve our community.

Who do you think has the political power in Lowell? Do you feel like the Cambodian community, given its size, is adequately represented politically?
We are definitely not adequately represented. We have to work on that more and have to learn how we can become leaders in our community.

Do you feel that the mainstream candidates are open to reach out to the Cambodian community?
I wouldn't say one hundred percent; but they are trying. Some members are trying to reach out to us and we are doing what we can to make ourselves be heard. Sometimes it's very difficult because we have such a small quiet voice in the community.

So your job as the president is political lobbying?
To lobby, to be a liaison, and to advocate for the Asian community.

Do you find it sometimes frustrating that there is no adequate political representation?

It is very frustrating because we do want someone in office to reflect the population, but we just can't get a candidate from the Asian community elected since former City Councilor Rithy Uong. We just don't have enough registered voters. We definitely need to promote voter registration more within our community. We also need to encourage potential candidates to put their name on the ballot. I'm not just speaking for the Cambodians I'm speaking for other minority groups as well.

Do you have potential candidates, but are you worried about the vote?
In the past we had different people run for School Committee and City Council, but we were unable to get enough votes to get them elected.

Is this due to the electoral system? Is that part of the problem? Or do people in the Cambodian community, which is typical for a lot of new immigrants, not like to vote? Is it sort of a double-edged sword in that sense?
It is double-edged. We have a lot of people who are not citizens and we have some U.S. citizens who are not registered to vote. We also have some who are registered to vote but do not vote. I wonder if having translation services available or diverse precinct/ward volunteers would help increase the number of voters.

How do you address that issue; or can you address that issue?
We are trying. We offer citizenship classes through CMAA. Other community agencies also try to encourage people to register to vote. We need to continue to encourage civic engagement in our community.

Does that sometimes frustrate you or do you think it's going to work itself out?
We have the numbers. All we need to do is to learn how to use them successfully. I'm hoping that in the future we'll be able to empower more folks to be more involved.

Other than Cambodians, would you like to see other groups represented in the city?
Yes, any minority group. I'm willing to support a strong candidate…someone who can be a positive role model for our young generation and who can inspire others to get involved.

Are there any efforts to make connections among different groups, say the African Cultural Association and the CMAA?
There was some discussion earlier about joining and taking part and making

connections with other minority groups in Lowell. We see this as a way to build strength and to motivate each other. And hopefully, maybe soon, we can make that happen. We can collaborate and be partners, so that together our voice can be heard.

Did you go to high school here in Lowell?
I actually didn't go to high school here; I went to the public vocational-technical high school in Tyngsboro.

That's close enough. What are your overall impressions about the educational opportunities in Lowell?
I think we have a great opportunity to do very well in Lowell. I mean this is a city where you can begin your education in pre-school and be able to graduate with a doctorate degree without having to leave it. This is an asset for us. As long as students stay focused and put in their best effort, they can be successful.

Have you done some of your university education in town or did you...?
I went to UMass Lowell.

When you were going to school here, were there bilingual programs? Khmer classes being offered? Those kinds of things? I think that has all changed recently?
It has changed. I did not get to participate in a bilingual program because when I came to Lowell, I was already a sophomore in high school.

Did they offer Khmer classes?
No, there weren't any Khmer classes.

Has that changed now?
Lowell High School has Khmer language classes available to students now.

Do you feel that there is an effort within the school system to respect the cultural identities of Cambodians and other immigrant groups?
I think we are doing a lot more to learn about the cultures that are in front of us in the classroom. And I think we are trying to be more sensitive to the needs of our diverse students. Teachers are taking courses and are participating in trainings in order to improve their instructional strategies and to improve their understanding of their students' backgrounds.

Was this the same when you were a student in the system?

No, I don't think so. I mean, like I said earlier, I didn't experience elementary and middle school education here. What they had in the past was a bilingual education program, where students received instruction in both their native language and English. Now it's different. We no longer have bilingual education. We have English Language Education Programs where students receive sheltered English language support, in most cases, in the mainstream classrooms.

And that's because of the state policies and the school system has to comply with those?
Right!

Do you feel that there's an adequate presentation of Cambodians and Southeast Asians in general, in the museums? Or would you like to see more?
I don't think so. I mean there were some displays at the Mogan Cultural Center, but not enough to represent the need of the community. I think it would be great if the National Park in the future could get more Southeast Asians involved and showcase more exhibits to highlight art, history, and culture of Southeast Asians.

How do you feel about the Park conducting tourism in the neighborhood, such as the walking tour through the Acre?
We had some thoughts on it. We think it would be a great idea to showcase Lowell's diversity. The only way for people to see the full diversity of Lowell is to tour different sections of Lowell and to be able to taste different foods or to be able to shop in different stores.

Have you experienced any racism or discrimination in the past or present here in Lowell? How does it feel being a Cambodian-American in the city?
I try not to take notice because if I notice this, it makes me feel sad and uncomfortable. So I try to ignore it and pretend that everything is good, and everything is safe. But I know that racism and discrimination exist. The only thing I can do in this situation is to be calm about it and try to be friendly with people. I know that to change the course of racism and discrimination, we need to educate our community about the different cultures here. I think that would help eliminate or decrease racism and discrimination. I also think that when a person has a negative attitude about a group or an individual, it's mostly based on misconceptions and misunderstandings. If people have a chance to learn about the history and cultures of others, they may develop sensitivity, compassion and

tolerance. We need to dispel our fears and apprehensions and learn to embrace and appreciate our unique differences.

How do you think Lowell has changed since you came here in the mid-1980s?
Lowell has changed a great deal especially in the downtown and Acre area. Before, our family used to live in the Acre. My parents opened up their grocery business in the Acre in 1987. My memory of the Acre back then was of violence and fear. We had gangs and drugs in the area. The city cleaned up the area a great deal. Taking down old and abandoned buildings and developing new ones.

Do your parents still run the grocery store?
No, they sold it in the mid-1990s.

So they are retired now?
Yes, they've just recently retired.

How is that working out for them? Do they like it, or?
I'm not sure. My mother is still thinking about pursuing another business when she comes back from visiting Cambodia.

What dreams do you have for your future, for yourself, for the city, for Cambodia, for the United States?
Right, for the whole world [Both laugh]. Well, for Lowell, for our community, I hope that in the future we'll be able to have more multicultural activities, collaborations, and partnerships. I think in order for us to live together more peacefully, we need to have all of that; we need the opportunity to get to know each other so that we can grow together. And for Cambodia, I dream for peace, stability and democracy.

If you were there to ask a question about the experience of immigrants in Lowell, what would it be? Or in other words, what is the question I should have asked you but I didn't ask you?
I think questions about adaptation and background. Lowell is known historically as a city of immigrants. In order to help immigrants and refugees transition smoothly and successfully in our society, we need to understand the adaptation process and the different background experiences that newcomers bring with them to Lowell. Through my own experience as a newcomer, I learned that when a newcomer arrives with strong educational background and strong skills that are

transferable in his/her new setting, he/she is able to adapt quicker.

As we are learning, this is not the case for many newcomers. Most of them arrived here with trauma, with fear, uncertainty and limited skills making adjustments and adaptation an every-day struggle. As a community, we need to work together and help encourage each other to become successful citizens.

So how do you think that your background has influenced your experience? [Phala laughs] I am just developing your question now. [Both laugh]
How did my background influence my experience? Hmm, I came here at a very young age so I was able to go to school, learn English and learn a set of skills that were very different from my parents. So I was very thankful for that opportunity. I think being able to survive the ordeal of the Khmer Rouge has made me a more resilient, more sensitive, and more compassionate person. I feel that I can try many new things and be able to survive them all because nothing can compare to the Khmer Rouge experience.

How do you think your parents' background... because maybe they were urban, because they already knew a little bit French— I am just recapturing the things you mentioned— how might that have shaped their experience? I know it's hard to talk for your parents.
My father, before the Khmer Rouge era was a teacher. And my mother was a business woman. So when they came here, they couldn't use their skills and degree. My father didn't have enough English to teach when he arrived here, so he had to start all over again doing whatever jobs he could find at that time. And for my mother, we didn't have the money to open up a business when we first arrived here, so she also had to start from scratch doing odd jobs.

I believe my parents made three dollar and twenty-five cents per hour when they started working in 1981. My mother sewed fur coats and my father worked as a nurse's assistant in a nursing home. My parents worked hard and managed their incomes wisely and were able to save enough money to buy a car a year later. Once they learned enough English and were able to find their way around town, they were able to acquire better jobs. From there, we continued to work hard as a family and saved enough to realize some of our American dreams.

Thank you for your time and sharing your family's and your personal story with us. We very much appreciate it.

CHAPTER THREE

Gordon Halm

Gordon, a husband and father of three sons, migrated to Lowell in the 1990s. He is a Ghanaian who lived in Liberia for a time. Gordon is an active member of Lowell's Ghanaian and African communities and has organized and co-organized various important cultural events in the city. He is the recipient of numerous awards for his work in the community. He also directs a project to support an Anglican school in his Ghanaian hometown of Winneba. Christoph Strobel interviewed Halm, an Elder at the Eliot Presbyterian Church in Lowell, on January 16, 2008.

> I consider Winneba my home. It's the town where I was born and where I grew up. Winneba happens to be in Ghana, and that will be my first home. Lowell is my second home because this is where I live now. This is where all my kids were born. I'm part of the community. We are very productive citizens of Lowell. We consider Lowell as our second home.

My name is Gordon Halm and I am originally from Ghana. I was born in a town called Winneba. Winneba is about 35 miles from Accra, which is the capital of Ghana. I left Winneba to go to Liberia where I met my wife. Before the civil war in Liberia started, my wife had an opportunity to come to the United States, because her brother was here, and he invited her to come. That was in 1989 shortly after the civil war started. I was in Liberia, and you can just imagine what it's like when there are gunshots here and there every day. But with the help of some friends I was able to get out.

How did you get out of Liberia?
At the time the rebels had not taken the airport. I was able to get help from friends

and board a plane. When I came to the U.S., I was living with friends in New York City. At that time my wife and I had no contact. Through my New York friends I located her phone number and I called her and she told me she lives in Lowell and invited me to join her. That was in 1995.

Aside from the Liberian community in the city, there is also a pretty big Ghanaian community in Lowell? At the Eliot Church there seems to be a lot of people from Ghana. I happen to be an elder at the Eliot Church. A while back, I started an independence celebration service at the Eliot Church. Our Independence Day falls on March 6. Every sixth of March I invite friends from Ghana and other African countries to come celebrate our independence through prayers and stuff like that. Through that the Ghanaian community became connected. Now we have an established group called the Ghanaian Community of Greater Lowell. I don't know if you remember, or might have heard, but last year was the 50th anniversary of Ghana's independence. We organized a huge program at city hall. And our community is growing.

Here at the University— it's tangentially relevant to the topic, or maybe just out of curiosity— a former Ghanaian student of mine gave this wooden carving to me. But she lives in Worcester and I've had a series of students from Ghana who live in Worcester. Do you interact with the Worcester community at all? In Massachusetts we have the Ghanaian Association of Greater Boston, which comprises all the Ghanaians in the state. I happen to be the second Vice President of that association. When we have programs a lot of people come from Worcester. There are Ghanaians all over Massachusetts, but the largest group is in Worcester. I think there's about five thousand or so.

Since your wife is Liberian, do you interact more with the Liberians or the Ghanaians? Or does it not matter? I lived in Liberia. I have traveled to Nigeria. I have connections and interact with everyone. It doesn't matter if they're Ghanaian, Liberian, Sierra Leonean... I have a lot of friends from Cameroon, Liberia, Uganda, and I work at the African Assistance Center. So I happen to see a lot of Africans from many countries.

Obviously the civil war was what pushed you to come to the United States. Did you have any preconception about America before you came to the U.S.?

Oh yes, big time! When we were in Africa we saw America as the land of milk and honey, and I think the media also portrays that message to us. We think the U.S. is the land of opportunity, and yes it is. But the idea we had was that things were so easy here. Once you are here, you have a different mindset altogether about what you perceive this country to be. Though this country, no question about it, is the greatest country on earth, but you have to work extremely hard for what you need here. It's different.

Is it hard when you interact with family back in Liberia and Ghana, because they think you live in the U.S. and this is the "land of milk and honey"?
One cannot know it or understand it until you get here. We tell them that this is a great country, but everything we have, we have to work for. You know in Africa, though people are very busy, you can't compare it to this place. Here if you don't pay your mortgage for a month or two, the next month you are out, but over there time is not that precious. But over here because I know I have an interview at eleven I have to be there by eleven, back there it's different. Over here we are more programmed, more time conscious and we have to move faster. Life in Africa moves a little bit at a slower pace. It is more relaxed.

How long have you lived in Lowell and whereabouts do you live in Lowell?
I've lived in Centralville for over thirteen years.

Do you own the place?
Gordon: Yes.

Do you consider yourself as being part of the Centralville neighborhood?
Yes. In the past I used to attend the neighborhood meetings on Monday nights. We would go there and raise concerns and issues in our neighborhood. But since I went back to school and with work, I haven't had a chance to attend the meetings lately. We consider ourselves part of the neighborhood. Although about two years ago, it was on Sunday, we were getting ready to go to church and when we came outside our minivan was gone. Someone had broken into and had vandalized our cars before. People threw eggs at our building. We kept reporting all these issues until someone came and stole the car. When that happened we were devastated. We were saddened that someone could possibly do this. We were not sure who was behind these incidents.

My wife and I have three sons, eleven, nine, and four years old, and we get along with our friends and neighbors. It was such a difficult time for us. But the Lowell police and officials supported us through the ordeal and they assured us it wasn't race related. At the time we felt that it was, because the perpetrators had come and done graffiti. It was pretty scary.

The kids were scared. We were scared ourselves that this could happen to us. But with the help of the police, they took the matter very seriously. The news, Channel 7, came to our house and covered the story. We had people calling us from Boston and everywhere because they saw my wife and me on television. That's where we really felt the support of the community and not only the Ghanaians. People wrote letters to the mayor and the chief of police. We felt that if you have connections with neighbors and friends, it goes a long way.

Did you experience other forms of discrimination or racism similar to that?
Our neighbors are all white and Spanish. Sometimes when they go on vacation they give us their keys. That's how it is. When the trash man comes and the barrels are in the street, before you know it, they come and take our barrel to our back yard. And all of a sudden we had people breaking into our car, throwing eggs at our house, and all of that. At the time we felt we were being targeted. But as of today, whoever is behind the attacks, we don't know and the police still don't have answers. The van was recovered about a week after we made the report, and it had been burned on the inside.

The saddest thing about it was the way the insurance company handled the whole issue. I think they must have felt that we had something to do with the incident. The rental car that they were supposed to provide, they weren't giving it to us. They were not forthcoming. They told us to go and find a lawyer for an examination under oath, or whatever they call it. My wife and I told them we were not going to get a lawyer and pay even one cent to a lawyer to defend us.

We bought our car. Somebody stole it and burned it to ashes, and we have to take a lawyer and do an examination under oath? We were really upset. We felt very discouraged, saddened, and we didn't take the lawyer. We went to the examination and they asked us where our lawyer was. We told them that we don't need a lawyer. They asked us if we were prepared for this and I said yes, and we sat down.

For about two hours they were asking questions and later on they told us that they noticed some stuff and would call back to get additional information and I said whatever additional information they needed I would provide it. They said it would take about a week to get back to us and I said okay. The next day my cell phone rang. I picked up the phone and one of the insurance detectives mentioned his name and he said they just wanted to apologize for what we have been going through, the emotional stress, and all of that. They had just found out that we had nothing to do with that.

So, you've had good times and bad times.
Good times and bad times, yes. As immigrants we certainly do. I know everyone has his or her story and this is our story. We haven't moved. We are not afraid. We still live in the same place and we still get along with our neighbors.

There are more and more people of African descent moving to Pawtucketville and Centralville right?
Yes.

Do you feel that's helping? Does the greater visibility help, or does it make things worse?
We haven't really heard of anybody else from Africa being attacked. The attacks were a difficult moment for us as a family. It makes you afraid to go home. What is going to happen next? Time has healed the emotional stress. I even had to quit my job because of that. I would be at work and the insurance company would call, the police would need us. It was a lot.

So your employer wasn't happy to accommodate that?
No, I quit on my own. I was a supervisor in a nursing home?

Is that when you started working for the African Cultural Association?
No, I had two jobs, as many immigrants do. You cannot make it on one job. So I quit the other job that I had and stayed with what I am still doing. That way, during the day when the insurance or the police called, I could be available to go right away. It was very stressful.

So currently you work two jobs?
I work at Life Links. We work with people with developmental difficulties. For the past year and a half I had a part-time job at the African Assistance Center where we help Africans who come to Lowell find resources in the city. I am currently an

undergraduate at UMass Lowell. Since I started school… it's difficult to maintain that. So I left the African Assistance Center, but I go there to volunteer whenever they need me.

And your wife is working too?
She graduated from UMass last year in June and got a B.A. in developmental disabilities. She also works with Life Links. My major is psychology. I would like to become a community psychologist. That's what I'm hoping to have my Master's Degree in; that's what I'm working towards now.

Do you still have parents and grandparents that live, in your case, in Ghana and in your wife's case, in Liberia?
I have lost both parents, and my wife's father got killed during the Liberian civil war, but her mother and other siblings were able to make it to Ghana, so they are in Ghana at the moment.

Are they in one of the refugee camps there?
When they went at the beginning they were in the refugee camp, but now they've been relocated to a different town. So that's where they're living now, in the eastern part of Ghana.

Are they thinking of going back to Liberia?
The conditions… just imagine ten years of civil war. Bodies burnt to ashes and people don't even know, can't even find their relatives, their family. Some people have lost their entire family. I know it is difficult. Some people are visiting. People are going back, but not necessarily to settle. People are going back to survey and all of that. But I know eventually people will go back, though at this point people mostly go there for visits.

Where do you consider your home? Is it Lowell, Ghana? Liberia?
I consider Winneba my home. It's the town where I was born and where I grew up. Winneba happens to be in Ghana, and that will be my first home. Lowell is my second home because this is where I live now. This is where all my kids were born. I'm part of the community. We are very productive citizens of Lowell. We consider Lowell as our second home.

Do you think of going back to Ghana at some point when you're older, maybe to retire?

Yes, I would like to go back. Technology is improving things. We can call Africa any time of the day now, unlike before when you could not access a phone line. But even though we talk to them, it's not like seeing them. I haven't seen my family in a long, long time.

Have you been able to go back at all since you came here?
No.

That must be really hard.
It is hard. Hopefully, in the future, we'll be able to take the children.

What ethnic background in Liberia is your wife from?
Actually, her parents migrated from Ghana to Liberia and were naturalized citizens of Liberia. Even though she was born and raised there she remained connected to her Ghanaian roots. We blend very well.

Do you try to educate your children in terms of teaching them your native language, songs, or culture?
It's sad. Sometimes I sit down and wish my children could speak my native language. I do blame it on me as a parent. My wife would take part of the blame and I would take part of the blame. If we had spoken the language at home and kept speaking it every day since they were born they would be able to speak it. Right now they understand, but can't speak. I also think that has to do with the day care they went through and the school system and all that. When we dressed them in traditional African attire, let's say for Sunday school, or whatever, they felt very uncomfortable, like they are sticking out. That was until the festival began.

The African Festival?
Yes, I have to tell you how it began. When I started the Ghanaian Independence service at our church many of the people from other African countries would be invited too. After the church service we had music and dance and people brought all kinds of food and all that. I thought if I'm able to put all this together, why don't we create a festival? All of the people from different African countries would come together and showcase their culture, music, and food. That's how the festival came about. And our kids, when they went to the festival and they saw other kids wearing traditional attire, they became proud to wear it.

You talked a little bit about being an elder in the Eliot church. What role does the church play in your life, and what role does the Ghanaian community play in your life?
I think the church is a good place to go. Back in Africa I went to Anglican school, and the church and the school were connected. Every Sunday we had to be in the church. The church is where we learned to differentiate between good and evil. The church is considered the place where a child will be trained in a good way so that when he or she grows up they will not deviate from good Christian teachings. The Eliot church has embraced the African community, Cambodians, Brazilians, etc. So when we go to church the spiritual peace is there. We go and worship our creator and it's also an opportunity where we can, as church members and friends, communicate and also help one another.

For example, if I lose my job, and I have a friend to talk to that friend might have an opportunity to speak to his supervisor and make a recommendation. So the church is where we go for our spiritual growth and also where we have a social network. When things happen to you, the church is there; the whole congregation is there. It is emotional and spiritual support.

Why the Eliot Church?
I went to Eliot church because of my wife. Her background is Presbyterian. When she came to Lowell in 1989, there were all the African community churches around here. But she had this strong Presbyterian background. So when I came here, obviously, I had to worship where she worshipped. That's how I became part of the Eliot church.

The Eliot church is very active in the community with the Thanksgiving feast and so on.
For the past few years, I have been the coordinator of that. We serve meals to about three hundred to four hundred homeless. During Thanksgiving last year, for instance, the amount of turkey, and also the people, not necessarily from our church, but from the community, they will call the church and our pastor and the secretary will forward the message to me. It might say we have a group from this place that would like to volunteer and leave their name and I will call them. It's very touching. It's amazing. People will cook the turkey and bring it, bring pies. So the church is very connected to the community, and when the homeless come you see them all lighten up. Thanksgiving is one of the positive things that the church continues to do for the community.

Have you ever had family come here from Liberia or Ghana to visit you, or is that not feasible?

It is not common for a family member to visit, because you have to get a visa issued and you have to go through a whole lot of requirements. If you don't meet the requirements your visa is denied. But what has been helpful as of late is that we have the green card lottery. If a family member plays and happens to win, then you have the chance of getting here. That has helped a lot of immigrants to come to the United States. Wars obviously too pushed people to migrate from Liberia, Sudan, Congo, and other places.

Let's talk a little bit about power and politics in Lowell. Do you think there is a fair representation of the African community in Lowell? Do you feel like people on the city council reach out to the African community?

I would say that city hall is our home and the city officials, the current mayor, Bill Martin, (editor's note: Bill Martin is no longer mayor of Lowell. Lowell's city council elects a new mayor every two years and has a professional city manager who runs it day-to-day.) He (Martin) is a very good friend and very supportive. And all the councilors, Councilor Rita Mercier and Bud Caulfield, they very much have the interests of the African community at heart. Whenever there is a program and we invite the mayor or the city councilors and all that, if their schedule permits, they will come and support it. And just imagine! On our Independence Day we go to city hall to do a flag raising. So at city hall the Ghanaian flag is flown in the sky for a week or two. I think that's pretty incredible. Driving by Merrimack Street you see the Ghanaian flag, the Liberian flag and all that.

Would you like to see more representatives that are Cambodians, Africans, Vietnamese, Brazilians, etc.?

It is our community's dream that we will see one of us as a city councilor. But it does take an individual to take that on. You can't just become a city councilor in a daydream.

Do your children go to public school?

My kids, like I said we have three boys, and we started them in a private school nearby our house. But there came a time when tuition was too expensive. We have moved the sixth grader and the fourth grader to the new charter public school. That's where they go now. We have a kindergartener who is still in private school.

Are you happy with the quality of the public schools in town?
The school is good. So far the kids have not had any major problems. The teachers, the administration, they have the well-being of the kids as their priority. They make sure the kids take their reading very seriously. Also the new school is more diverse. The private school had only a few minorities. At the charter school you have Cambodians, Spanish, and Africans. So when we go over there we see more diversity.

Even though the private school had stricter discipline, it didn't mean that the kids were always better behaved. It's a good school and the teachers are always on top of the kids if there are any concerns or issues they will call or arrange a meeting to see how best to resolve whatever the situation is. I went through a public school and public schools made me who I am today. I think the important thing is for parents to stay on top of their kids and stay involved with the school.

Do you participate in PTA meetings?
Yes, they call it PET. Last year we went to the State House in Boston because the state cut funds from the public school. We petitioned them to stop cutting the funds. My wife and I went. We go to association meetings as well.

So what are your dreams for yourself and your family, for the city, for your life? What are your dreams and aspirations as you continue your life?
Well, my dream is always to do the right thing, to stay healthy, and also to complete my MA in community psychology, because I see myself reaching out to the disadvantaged to make a difference in someone's life. I would like to see my kids grow up to become good citizens wherever they are. It is my hope that the children have better lives, that the parents are more focused on their children so we can all live in peace.

So the last question is, since we're not perfect, is there one question you think I should have asked you and I didn't ask you?
You know, you could have asked me: Have I made a difference in someone's life? I think about five years ago, while working my overnight job, I thought about how I started school. I was walking barefoot, two miles back and forth. Now here are my kids going to school with backpacks, books, and all that. I thought my kids are very, very lucky. That's not what I went through. I went to the bank and took a hundred dollars and I bought a money order and I sent it to Ghana, to Winneba,

my former school, the Anglican Primary School. I sent it to my brother to send it to the school, to the head master, to help the school buy furniture or help people to pay their fees and all that.

We have been helping the school ever since and currently we are doing a two classroom block. We have sent computers, and they have sent us pictures of the kids, they have a video, reporters went to the school and they sent me that. And if you see kids wearing a school uniform, with the little money we sent over, everybody has chairs, and all that. And that alone goes a long way for us. They send us pictures and all that. I think if you have the means to help someone, definitely do it. I don't care if it is one penny I will give it to make the other person's life better, so we can all live, because you never know what's going to happen. What goes around comes around.

Thank you very much!

CHAPTER FOUR

Thong Phamduy

Thong Phamduy came to the United States as a refugee from Vietnam. A husband and father, he works as an educator. Thong plays a leading role as a community activist in the Vietnamese community. He created a vibrant Vietnamese language program at St. Patrick's Church and is a co-creator and co-organizer of the Vietnamese New Year celebrations. Christoph Strobel interviewed Thong on April 30, 2008.

I was accepted at UMass Lowell after one year of community college. That brought me to Lowell. I saw during my time here that the cost of living seemed fairly affordable. I worked my way through college. In the summertime I worked a lot of jobs. I was able to save and to purchase a home back then to share with my brother and sister. That's one of the big reasons why I continued to stay. But there's another reason. Some people tend to move out of Lowell when they settle, or when they start to make their career. I wanted to stay in Lowell and continue to work and invest in the city. I did a lot of work around here.

My name is Thong Phamduy. I've lived in the lower Highlands, for probably about twenty years there now. Previously I lived in South Lowell, for about five years there. So I lived a total of twenty-five years in Lowell.

You came here from Vietnam? Can you talk a little bit about your experience if you don't mind?
Most of the Vietnamese who got out of the country between 1975 to, I would say 1990, or even a little later than that, got out by boat. They're called "Boat People."

I was part of the first wave of boat people, those who left during the first five years after the collapse of Saigon. A big wave of people got out by boat. Usually we landed in another country near Vietnam, in my case Indonesia. Other people landed in the Philippines or Malaysia. We basically waited there and hoped that another country would accept us as refugees. In my case the U.S. picked me up.

How long did you stay in the refugee camps?
Probably about six months.

That was relatively fast then.
Very short! The refugees during the first wave could still relatively easily leave for a third country.

What motivated you to leave Vietnam?
We had to get out. The Communists took over, and my family, we had ties with the old government. My father was working for the police force. He was a high ranking officer. So we had a difficult time. He was jailed. That was the main reason. We couldn't live there; it was just too difficult.

Were you able to leave with your entire family or did you have to split up?
For most of the boat people it was very difficult to get the whole family out. Luckily I was able to bring three of my sisters with me. I'm the oldest one in a family of eight.

There are a lot of horrible stories about the experience of the boat people. Pirates, bad weather...
Our trip was so lucky. We spent about four days and four nights at sea until we landed. It was a very smooth trip.

Were the conditions on the boat really crowded?
Very crowded! Just imagine a thirty-foot boat that fit 105 people.

One hundred and five on a thirty foot-long boat, wow! It must have been a scary experience?
We decided to either get out of the country or die. There was no other choice, but people were scared.

Was Lowell the first city you arrived at in the United States?
No, I ended up in Salem, Massachusetts [about thirty miles from Lowell and near Boston]. That was my first place. We got there in 1980.

What made you decide to come to Lowell?
I got accepted at UMass Lowell as a college student, and I brought everybody with me.

What subject did you study?
Mechanical engineering.

Is that the field you work in now?
No. I changed to education.

So you're teaching?
High school.

And that's in Malden?
In Malden.

Do you like that job?
As a matter of fact, I love to teach. When I came to this country, unfortunately, I couldn't pursue that, because my English back then was just terrible. So the only choice I had was to go into engineering, where there was less reading and writing. So I could survive.

After I finished my Bachelor's Degree, I think in 1985, I continued in graduate school. I got accepted at the Massachusetts Institute of Technology. I went there for three and a half years. Between the Master's Degree and the Ph.D., I got married and there were things I had to take care of.

Life happens.
Yes. So I got my Master's Degree and I got out. At the time my English had improved and I decided to change careers.

And then you went into education. Did you work in Malden the whole time?
Yes, for twenty-one years now. Ten years teaching and I'm an administrator now. I'm a District Director of Technology.

So you do a lot of teacher training and technology acquisitions and those sorts of things?
Everything! It started with a small department, basically support. Then we expanded the whole technology support, the Information Technology Department, database, and all of that. And now we also oversee the Parent Information Center. So that's a

part of the service I'm doing. Registration for new students, make sure the data and everything is going smoothly.

What was your first impression when you came to the United States?
I felt just really blessed.

Was the fact that there is a fairly sizeable Southeast Asian Community in Lowell, did that attract you to the city? Or was it school?
It was just a matter of coincidence. I was accepted at UMass Lowell after one year of community college. That brought me to Lowell. I saw during my time here that the cost of living seemed fairly affordable. I worked my way through college. In the summertime I worked a lot of jobs. I was able to save and to purchase a home back then to share with my brother and sister. That's one of the big reasons why I continued to stay. But there's another reason. Some people tend to move out of Lowell when they settle, or when they start to make their career. I wanted to stay in Lowell and continue to work and invest in the city. I did a lot of work around here.

I was told you are active in the Vietnamese Community?
I'm very active. We are a small community. We are not large like the Cambodians. If you are talking about Asians, yes, there's a big Asian Community in Lowell. But when you start to break it down you will find that 80-90 percent are Cambodians. Then you got the Laotian and Vietnamese. I think we got a few thousand Vietnamese… I am very involved with the community. When I was a student at UMass, I set up the Vietnamese Student Club or Association. And then from that time on we got together to organize the celebration.

Which celebration are you referring to?
The New Year's Celebration. When I became the president of the Vietnamese Student Association, I started to get the community involved, to get everyone to come and celebrate. We were using Cumnock Hall. And that event continues until now. We also organized the Vietnamese Catholic Group—about twenty people when we started out.

Which church are you involved with?
Saint Patrick's.

And you guys meet in the basement there I heard?

Correct. That has become a magnet to Vietnamese for all kinds of activities.

And people who show up for that, they are not necessarily Catholic?
No it's not necessary to be Catholic.

Do you go to Vietnamese stores or restaurants for food?
I don't think there is any Vietnamese market here. But we do have numerous Vietnamese restaurants around. They are all great. My family actually started a restaurant here, the first one in Lowell.

Which one is that?
It has changed names. It was Viet Thai Palace on Drum Hill. We started that restaurant, and we operated it for three years. We were not good at business. So it did not last. We transferred it to other people and they continued. Actually a friend of mine runs it.

Is it Pho 88 now?
Pho 88!

Do you have children?
Oh yes, five.

Do you still have relatives back in Vietnam?
As I mentioned to you, I had brought three sisters with me. Then two more siblings joined us a year later. Probably about six years later the other two got out, also by boat. All eight of us got out. My parents remained in Vietnam. When I became a citizen I sponsored my parents. That was ten or fifteen years ago when my parents came over. We reunited the whole family, except cousins of course. They're still there, but other than that everybody is here.

Are you still in touch with your cousins at all, or not so much?
Not too much, only once in a while.

Is most of your extended family still living in Lowell, or have your siblings moved to other places.
We love to be near each other so we can support each other. We make our decisions together. We tried to stick together in Lowell, unless, you couldn't find a job around here. Then you had to move. There are only two siblings who moved out to California because of jobs. But the rest are still in Lowell.

That is great!

We still get together every weekend. And then it all centers on community work. I started a Vietnamese Language Program eleven years ago. Now that program seems to meet the needs of a lot of Vietnamese people. We have about 100 students in the program and ten teachers. We run thirty weeks per year starting in September. Like the school year. The students usually stay in our program between eight and ten years. It's a little bit at a time, but we show results.

Obviously it's very important for the community in general, but I imagine too for your children to learn Vietnamese.

That was the driving force behind the creation of the program. Because in my own family we have twenty some kids.

So you're basically trying to maintain and pass on Vietnamese culture to your kids through language, through celebrations like the New Year. Are there other things you do to maintain a Vietnamese cultural identity?

For my family we're using food and family weekend gatherings. We always eat Vietnamese food on the weekend. So it continues. We also go to Vietnamese restaurants.

Do you speak English with your children or Vietnamese?

Both.

How good are your kids with their Vietnamese?

Pretty good. The goal of the Vietnamese Family Program is for the youth to become instructors for the next generation, so that we are able to carry on that mission. As soon as they finish the program after eight years, usually eight years, they're invited to become a teaching assistant for two years or three years. Then they become instructors. Usually they instruct the lower classes. The elder like myself, we cover the upper classes including culture, poetry, and everything else.

That's pretty rigorous.

Since I'm a teacher I know how to create curriculum. I am able to work with the group and create our own curriculum. We are revising it every year. It is a working model.

This is very fascinating. Did you talk to other Vietnamese about that as sort of a model...or even other immigrants?

I tried to bring that model to some other communities for consideration. How do you make the program sustainable in this society? We try to preserve the language, but how do you do that? Of course, before I created this program I had to do some research about other programs. I learned from those models.

It's very remarkable. Does your wife work too?
Not with the five kids! We both were students. I met her at UMass Lowell. I was a senior, she was a freshman. Then I went on to graduate school. And then later on, we married, we've had children. So she quit in the middle to take care of the kids. She's a wonderful woman. After ten years out of school, she applied and she finished her Master's Degree about two years ago. After that she and I created a company. We write educational web applications.

Oh wow! So you're a teacher, administrator, community activist, creator of a company, husband, father of five, and you're a weekend teacher of Vietnamese.
Oh, that's just one small piece.

How much do you sleep?
Like you. [Both laugh] I love community work… Saint Patrick is one of the things I really enjoy. Not only for the Vietnamese aspects, but in general… it is a multi-ethnic parish.

There are often discussions about intergenerational conflict in immigrant communities, such as differences in values. Can you talk about that?
You find that often. However it depends on how you resolve that. Communication is a key thing. That's what we try to do in our community, and of course in my family. We try to have the youth take the lead in the community. This is very different from traditional Vietnamese culture.

Thank you so much for taking the time to talk with us. This was very insightful.

CHAPTER FIVE

Bowa Tucker

Bowa Tucker came to the United States from Sierra Leone in the 1970s. He works in Lowell at the UMass Lowell Center for Family, Work and Community where he directs a project with Lowell High School designed to make college a reality for students who likely will be the first in their family to go to college. A father and husband, he was interviewed by Christoph Strobel on January 10, 2008. Since this interview he earned his doctorate at UMass Boston in the field of educational leadership!

Tunnels amazed me. Those kinds of things I couldn't understand. And we would be driving on the highway and someone would point out the fact that we were driving under water and I still find that difficult to comprehend; how that can be possible?

The roads, the buildings, the stores, the skyscrapers, those things fascinated me, and then I found out that people are just people anywhere. There's no significant difference whether you're from a village or you live in the most advanced country in the world. I think human beings have the same fundamental needs and they're not that different.

Could you tell us a little bit about your migration history? Why did you decide to come to the United States? Why Lowell?

My father actually decided for my sister and myself to join him. He was already here in the United States. I was very young then. I think I was in my teens and he wanted us to join him, so he came back to Sierra Leone and got us.

Where were you from originally?
Sierra Leone.

Did your coming to the U.S. have to do with the civil war? Did your father want you out of the country because of that? Or was there no connection to that?
It was before [the war]. We came in the 1970s. At that time there was stability in the country, even though we had a leader who in many respects would have been considered a dictator, because we had a single party system. But there was no fighting. My mother and my father were here in the United States and we had stayed behind in Sierra Leone until they got fairly stable and then they decided we should join them.

Did your grandparents raise you at the time, or your aunts and uncles?
My uncle and his wife.

In Sierra Leone did you live in the city or the countryside?
It was on an island. I don't know if you're familiar with a map of Sierra Leone, but there's a little island called Bonthe and that's where I lived.

When you found out you would be moving to the United States did you have preconceived ideas about what it would be like coming here?
Oh yeah, at that time, most people aspired to come to the United States and I'm sure to a large extent people still do. It was viewed as paradise on earth, if there's any such a place. And so there was a lot of excitement about coming to America. I was absolutely ecstatic when I learned that we were going.

And did that bubble burst a little when you got here?
To some extent. Tunnels amazed me. Those kinds of things I couldn't understand. And we would be driving on the highway and someone would point out the fact that we were driving under water and I still find that difficult to comprehend; how that can be possible?

The roads, the buildings, the stores, the skyscrapers, those things fascinated me, and then I found out that people are just people anywhere. There is no significant difference whether you're from a village or you live in the most advanced country in the world. I think human beings have the same fundamental needs and they're not that different.

Did your family live in Lowell from the outset or did your family move around a little bit?
We moved around, but not for very long periods. My father actually lived in Philadelphia, PA. So that's where we met him. But at the time he was separated from my mother and my mother lived in Washington, D.C. So, I would go and visit my mom during the summers until my father decided to move to New York, in the Bronx. And I decided to stay with my uncle while I was in Philadelphia and I would visit either New York or D.C. Most of my moving around was really on the east coast, Washington, Philadelphia, New York, and occasional visits to Boston, that sort of thing.

So why and how did you eventually end up in Lowell?
Well, I was seeking employment. I went to college at Westchester University in Pennsylvania about thirty miles outside of Philadelphia. And when I graduated in 1984, I was seeking employment. My sister had been here [in Lowell] with her husband who was then a student at UMass Lowell. He was studying chemical engineering and the Massachusetts economy was very good at that time. It was the time of the "Massachusetts Miracle." The unemployment rate was very low. I think it went as low as four percent or so if not lower.

I had not succeeded in getting a job in Philadelphia, so my sister encouraged me to come and give it a shot here. So really that was the impetus for me to move here. Try and get a job. Initially, when I came, I was not impressed. Having lived in Philadelphia and coming to a place like downtown Lowell, there's no comparison especially if you look at the central business district and the buildings and different commercial enterprises. There's nothing here, and I was like, "What? And this is considered a city?" But surprisingly it's been nearly twenty-five years now and I'm still around.

When I think of Lowell now, I think of a fairly strong Sierra Leonean community. Was this already the case at the time or have you seen this growing?
It has gone through different phases. When I came here in the mid-1980s there were only maybe a handful of Sierra Leoneans, and those were primarily students. People did not come here to settle and raise a family. Some were here by virtue of being a student and decided not to leave afterwards. But because the economy was so good, and the health care industry in particular was hiring, a lot of immigrants ended up working in these elder care facilities.

We started to see a huge influx shortly after I came. Somebody knew somebody who knew somebody and then we started to see a gradual increase in the number of Sierra Leoneans. I don't know if Lowell went through a recession in the early 1990s or what have you, but we started to see a significant movement out of Lowell. People started to go elsewhere. But a good number still stayed and since then we've seen a very gradual migration from Lowell. It's not the number we had in the early to mid nineties. I would say from 1992 to 1996 a lot of people left.

Do you have any idea where they went?
Some people moved to New Hampshire, some moved to the suburbs, but not that many. I would say most moved out of state towards the Washington D.C.-Virginia area. Very recently a number of folks who left the community went to Ohio, because, I guess, Ohio is deemed very good as far as the cost of living and what-have-you.

It seems as if a lot of the migration out of Sierra Leone happened with the civil war?
Most of the current arrivals are what one would consider refugees, but prior to the civil war I think, especially for people who had the means to study abroad, they would generally send their children out to go and study. But I think during the civil war there were a lot of civil service agencies that helped process paper, refugee papers, to get people out of the war situation.

So a good number of folks left on that basis, but I don't think a lot of them settled here. You have families that have been here, but had relatives back there and I think that helped them to get their family out.

I want to switch to your life in Lowell and what that was like. Have you lived in Lowell since the mid-1980s?
Yes, I haven't moved out. I have grown to love Lowell and I live in the Greater Lowell area now. It's been almost twenty-five years.

When you were living in Pawtucketville, did you consider yourself as being part of that neighborhood? Were there African businesses you could go to, institutions like churches that you would attend, or was it just a place where you happened to live?
I initially lived in Centralville when I first moved to Lowell for a very brief time because I was staying with my sister and her husband, but then my first apartment was at Westminster Village, which is on Pawtucket Blvd going towards Tyngsboro. Westminster Village is a huge apartment complex. It's actually a village of its own

with a convenience store right there and some other small businesses at the plaza.

Then there's a church we used to attend, the Church of the Nazarene, which is walking distance from our apartment on Vernon Ave. During those initial periods, we didn't know a lot of people, so I can't say we were actively engaged in doing neighborhood or community kind of things. But as time went on…. The complex actually had a community center used by the residents for functions or whatever and we would use the center when we celebrated a kid's birthday, for example, and we would invite friends and some of the neighbors we knew. I can't say that outside of the people we knew, we went out of our way to know who our neighbors were or interact with them on a regular basis.

That makes sense. That's how most people live their life. Would you say that your circle of friends in the eighties and nineties were primarily Sierra Leonean, or were they neighbors and it didn't matter?

It was a mix. When we lived at thirteen-thirteen, we had a neighbor who lived downstairs from us. She has passed on. She was involved in an auto accident. We became friends. She was an Anglo woman. I don't know her ethnicity, for lack of a better word, but I know she had European heritage and we were very close with her. We would visit with her and she would come and visit with us. She had a daughter. But for the most part it was either Sierra Leoneans or folks from other African countries. People who lived in the complex were Ivorian, Cameroonian, and Kenyan. It was mostly people who were also African.

Are there African stores where you buy maybe groceries or music or whatever, or do you frequent the mainstream stores like Market Basket and Hannaford's?

We shop at both. For the most part I think we do most of our shopping at DeMoulas or Market Basket, but for certain special dishes, we do have a number of African stores that sell some of those items and we go there for those needs. For the longest time we would actually drive to Boston, Boston Tropical Food Market, and also Haymarket to do most of our shopping for food items.

Eventually, I don't recall if it was sometime in the mid-1990s or so, the first African store opened in Centralville by some Liberians who partnered and so we started to go there for some of those shopping needs. And then we just saw a growth of so many African stores, but I think for everyday shopping needs we still go to Market Basket and then for the special things we go to the African food stores.

What types of food do you eat most frequently?

Rice is our staple food. My ethnicity, I'm considered a Shabro, but we've been integrated so much into the Mende tribe that people think we're Mendes. If you go way back we're really Shabros, but the Mendes have dominated a lot of other groups. So, for the ethnic group that I belong to the food is cassava. A lot of cassava, a lot of plantain, yam, those kinds of food, but for a staple it's really rice.

Did you meet your wife in Lowell or while you were still in Pennsylvania?

She was home and I was here and we corresponded. We initially saw each other in New York.

Have you been able to go back to Sierra Leone?

Yes, I was there in 2002 last. I had been there prior to that as well. Maybe if things go well, I'll go visit again this year.

Do you still communicate with family back in Sierra Leone and if so, how do you do that?

Telephone. The cell phone, as you know being someone who studies Africa, is being used. Even the guy in the most remote village has a cell phone nowadays. We get a lot of calls. Communication has improved tremendously. Prior to the availability of cell phones, it was really hard to communicate through mail. Letter writing took months, but nowadays we can get calls on a weekly basis, and we do. Everybody needs something, so we send it.

Is there a lot of pressure to comply? I know with a lot of African friends that I have who live in the United States it is always a concern, all of these demands that need to be complied with. Is that sometimes strenuous?

It's very strenuous. I think it's something I particularly struggle with. On the one hand you want to be able to help people. On the other hand you need to be mindful of the fact you have your own family to worry about. And when people solely rely on you, then inasmuch as you want to help, at what point do you draw that line? So it's a big struggle for me.

I try to be helpful, but at the same time I ask myself, am I being really helpful by having someone solely dependent on me? What can I do to ensure that this person becomes self-sufficient? It's always a struggle.

I think it plays out on the ground too. I just spent some time in Senegal last summer and actually spent a good chunk of time in a village there. It's interesting to see that a lot of Senegalese are going to Spain now for work and the gap that is emerging in the community. Those members in the village who have family members abroad have a higher living standard. It seems to be creating some tensions in the communities there, so I understand your worries about sustainability, but on the other hand when someone asks you for help can you really…

It's a big struggle and on both sides. Not just my family, my wife's family as well. There's a lot of pressure on us to help folks and it's a big issue.

Do you have children?
Yes.

What would you like the future of your children to be like?
I really put a lot of emphasis on education. I would like to see them be college-educated, and to see them become responsible persons, not only for themselves, but also for society. So that's what I aspire to for them, to be of use to themselves and to society. It's equally hard when you raise kids who don't necessarily have the same vision that the parent might have. That can be very frustrating.

Do you feel there are some intergenerational tensions?
I think that's clearly an issue. I'm a very liberal person, but I think as one grows older, your values shift a little bit and you want to enforce some of that on your children, and they may not be in the same place as you. That creates some tensions. And what you may aspire for them may not jive with what they want, so trying to deal with that tension can be problematic at times. Not only that, but you mix in the cultural dimension, that of being raised here and coming from a different country, even though I was influenced a lot by this culture here, that creates tension as well.

Is there something that you would like your children to carry on from your family's background and beliefs? Do you teach them about their ethnic identity?
I guess to the best one can, I suppose. I wasn't raised in the village or in an environment where a lot of these traditions were really passed on to me. I think I missed out on some of that myself. But the ones that I am aware of I try to impart.

We do libation occasionally. Libation is, for example, when a loved one passes on, you do certain ceremonial things to acknowledge them, those sorts of things.

Whether they're going to practice that is another question and is not one we practice on a regular basis, but on occasion.

I also think that teenagers in mainstream society and in immigrant communities often seem to rebel a little. They might not do it now, but pick it up later, or they might be just complaining.

When they were a lot younger we used to do the African clothing so that they knew their parents came from a different place and that's how they dressed, but even with me, you'd never see me dressed like that anymore.

Any particular reason why?

I don't know if this has anything to do with identity, but I like a suit and tie. When I'm going to a wedding or important ceremonial things, and I don't know if this is in part being influenced by being here, but I've always just loved that all-male attire of wearing a suit and tie. I don't know if that's a European thing, or an American thing. Once in a while I will wear my African gowns, but it's just not something I do regularly like some folks.

Let me switch briefly to identity since you provided a nice transition. Identity questions are difficult because they're a multi-layered. Do you consider yourself African? American? African and American? Sierra Leonean? How does identity play out for you?

I'm an African living in America who has become American by nationality. But I am first and foremost, African born. That will never change, but I am an American citizen. I don't know if you would term that African-American or what.

It doesn't matter what I term it. It matters what you term it. Is it the same for your kids?

That's a good question and I don't think we've spent much time having that conversation in terms of how they see themselves. They are eighteen and seventeen and I think that they know their folks are African, but they were born here. They probably consider themselves American. But I think there's a link to the African heritage even though they've never been to Africa.

In Sierra Leone English was the main language, but did you also speak other languages when you were growing up?

Yes, I speak Mende, I speak Krio, which is like a broken English, Pidgin English, whatever they call it. Those were the two main languages. Then of course in school we learned how to speak English. But English was not used predominately outside of school. Krio was the main mode of communicating and Mende as well for us. But in school we had to learn how to speak English and that was what we spoke or tried to speak. And we would laugh at kids who spoke vernacular; who's English was not very proper in school.

In Senegal, for example, Wolof is becoming an important language compared to French. In Sierra Leone is Mende becoming the universal language or is Krio still the main language?
Krio is. It's the medium by which most people communicate. There are so many different tribes, let's say the majority will speak Krio, but you will not find tribes speaking the language of other tribes. It's just sort of the way things are.

Were you able to teach your kids some Krio and Mende?
They understand Krio and some Mende, but they don't speak it. We can communicate but they won't actually talk.

This is pretty common among immigrants in the United States. The children often understand because they hear their parents speak it, but they don't necessarily talk.
And I think that's a disservice to the kids really. In retrospect I wish I had been able to ensure that they were able to speak the language. And I think this is quite common especially among Africans, we make this move and make the mistake of not teaching our kids how to speak the native language. I think especially when they are very young they could acquire those things and we don't do it.

Do you think there's a particular reason for that? Is it a time issue?
Well, I think we don't think about it in those terms, because really when we think about language acquisition, at a very young age you start speaking and communicating to a child and the child responds. It doesn't really take extra time to teach the child.

I think we just really don't think about the importance of it. We get wrapped up in a society that speaks English and then we continue speaking English without thinking about where we're from and how we would like our kids to continue this language and the culture we came from. We don't think about that. There's not a conscious effort made by the majority of immigrants, especially African immigrants.

There are exceptions of course. There are some people who will make sure their kids learn their language, but I think by and large that is not the mode in which we think. And you know you're surrounded by television, radio, the influence and the impact of the dominant language, the mainstream. It's hard to deviate from that.

During your life in Lowell did you change jobs a lot?
During those initial years when I originally moved to Lowell I actually worked in health care taking care of the elderly. And I worked for an agency that sent me to different facilities, so in that sense I moved around a lot. But in another sense, I didn't leave health care and got into business and then from business to this or that, I pretty much stayed in that industry for a long time until I went to graduate school and studied community development and actually started doing community-related work.

What always impresses me about African immigrants is this drive for education for economic improvement and moral improvement.
We are raised to think that education is really what helps one to develop as a human being, and what can pave our way in society. So that's what's imparted to us at a really young age and we grow up thinking education is everything. Even at the expense of making money for some of us. So really in my case it creates a lot of problems because I'm always stressing it to my kids and to some extent there's rebellion that goes on because they don't see it the way I see it.

Education to me, because of the family I'm from, it's a priority, and I regret, I'm approaching almost fifty, and I would have loved to have had a PhD at a much younger age. But that's something that I'm still struggling for. Otherwise at my age why would I even bother? [Editors' note: Doctor Tucker earned his doctorate in 2010, about two years after this interview was completed!]

But it's really important, and I think it's one that transcends any economic benefit, because I could have used that money, learned how to invest in stocks and make a lot of money. But yet I choose to pursue education. So I don't know what drives that, but it's something that I value very much.

Is your wife working too?
Yes she is. She's a nurse.

Was she able to take some time off when your children were younger?
Not very much. I think she probably stayed home for six months with the first child. Then with the second child, we were fortunate to have her mother come to help us with the child at home. But then her mother ended up getting sick and we

had to take her back home where she passed away. So the kids didn't really grow up with grandparents, or having the external support from other family members. It was only always us. It was hard.

Does religion play an important role in your life? Is church important to you because it provides a social network as well as spiritual growth?

It is. I think more for spiritual growth than social networking. We go to a mainstream church and for some reason it's not the same here. People don't interact much. There's not that connectedness you would expect from people who go to the same place to worship. It is like everyone is on their own. We go for spiritual growth. To connect with people like one big happy family, that's missing and maybe that's because of where we go.

I think there are some other churches, especially within the African community, where that may be the case. I think they have a closer bond amongst the members of the congregation. But in the mainstream churches, I haven't found one that extends beyond "Hello," and that's it. It's almost like people are afraid to get too close to anyone.

Do you socialize much or do you not have much time for it?

No, I don't. At one point I was very actively engaged in the community. I spend a lot of time trying to organize within my own community. But I felt really burnt out by all that and I felt like what I was trying to do wasn't being appreciated by anyone else. So I think I've kind of retreated from all that and have become very conservative in the people I hang out with.

I could probably count on one hand the number of people I could call really close friends, partly because I'm busy, and also maybe because I'm influenced by the way things are in this society in terms of individualism. I don't bother with that anymore, I'd rather stay home alone and read a book or watch television or listen to music than call up friends and hang out over a beer and just talk. Maybe part of that is a personality thing.

Are there any particular TV programs you like to watch or any special type of music you like?

Oh yes. I love African music, I love reggae. I like to watch the news of course and every once and a while I watch Link TV. I don't know if you know Link TV. They do a lot of non-mainstream type journalism just to give you a different perspective from what the mainstream reports.

I don't have cable.
I know cable is something that can be expensive, but there are some really good television programs, Animal Channel is one. You learn about the way they live and see there's not a lot of differences between the ways human beings live. And also on Link TV I've learned a lot of different things, like about the link between slavery from East Africa to the Arab world. I didn't know about that history. There was one program on that and it was real eye opening to me. So there's a lot one can learn from documentaries and those sorts of things on television.

Do they have good African news coverage? Do you still keep up with what's going on in Sierra Leone?
I don't actively seek it out. At one time I did, because with the Internet now it's accessible, but somehow I'm not engulfed in it. I like to read African news produced by the BBC.

On their web page?
Yeah. But there's a publication too on African News; I get that at Barnes & Noble. It informs me about what's going on, on the continent. But that's the extent of it.

Do you get visitors from Sierra Leone at all?
Occasionally. Last year, my wife's uncle who had been Vice President [in Sierra Leone], visited us.

I remember that. I went to hear him speak!
Every now and then we'll get a relative, but that doesn't happen frequently.

How long do folks usually stay when they come?
A couple of weeks. We've never had a long-term visitor.

Do you take them to any particular places, or do you just chill at home with them, or do both?
We do both. We like to take them to learn about the city, go to Boston, that sort of thing. I like to go to the Kennedy Library every now and then with visitors.

Do you do stuff with the National Park here in Lowell at all?

Now that is an interesting question, and part of that is because as human beings we are always looking beyond our immediate neighborhood and community and sometimes we don't realize the really important and valuable things that are right next to us. So I think it's more based on that than anything else.

Do you think, if there were more African related exhibits, like on African immigration, would that entice you to go and visit?
I think so. I know that at one time Middlesex [Community College] had some affiliation with the New England Folk Life Center? I don't know if there was some funding that came through and they were trying to create some folk life center that would engage people from different cultures into doing different things and learning about different cultures, but we did a number of things with them.

Demonstrating how to prepare food that came from Sierra Leone and we also tried to bring in an exhibition to Lowell, the Gullhas. I don't know if you're familiar with The Gullhas. But they're African Americans from the [South Carolina sea] islands, and we were trying to bring that here. So I think if folks are more connected with stuff that relates to them there would be more involvement.

Are you involved with the African cultural festival?
Yes. I was one of the committee members that initially planned the first one and I have stayed connected to it. Every now and then I have served as the Master of Ceremonies, so yes, I'm very connected to it.

Are you registered to vote and do you generally vote in elections?
Yes.

Do you think, as a person of African descent living in Lowell, that people are politically representing you? That mainstream politicians reach out to the African community and try to find out what your needs are?
I think a number of politicians on the council, I can't say all, do acknowledge this population outside the mainstream, and want to hear their voices and to be able to represent them. I know for example, Bill Martin and Rita Mercier, when she was mayor before, would always be at the flag raising ceremony when the city allows different countries to showcase their flag on a given day that's important in their history. And they would always be there.

Beyond that, I can't say. But I think if people make their needs known to people who are in power, I think there might be some effort made to try to address them. If you're talking about the candidates actually taking the initiative to go out and reach out, then that depends upon the individual.

Do you feel that the people in the immigrant communities need to be more politically active on their end too?
Yes.

Do both sides "drop the ball" in a sense?
I think so. People who are in power will always be receptive to people who want their issues addressed, especially if they know it translates into votes. But I think the community as a whole, either they recognize the importance of it, and don't exercise it, or they just don't know. There really isn't much engagement with what is happening in the political arena of the city. And I think that is really to be put on the community because society encourages that you know. I know part of my frustration in trying to organize the community was based around that. There was no sense of civic responsibility. Everything has to be connected to a "what's-in-it-for-me" mentality. It doesn't always work like that. So it was very hard.

I think I was probably well poised to emerge as a potential candidate for the city council, if I had really pushed for it. I had been very active in a number of neighborhood activities across the city when I worked for the city of Lowell as Assistant Director of Neighborhood Services. We used to provide services to all neighborhoods in the city so I became well known. If I had aspired for public office to that extent, I'm pretty confident that I would have made it. I hope that doesn't sound too arrogant! What I'm trying to say is that sometimes we as a community don't take on the responsibility of trying to provide support or services within our own community. Part of that has to do with the level of frustration we feel when we try to do that, and that discourages us.

Would you like to see more immigrants on the city council?
I think it only makes sense. Given the demography of the city it naturally makes sense. When I used to represent the city at the "All-America City" competition—which was a competition put forth by Allstate to recognize cities that had actively engaged their residents in public life—the question that always emerged was who would go and represent the city. And the judges would say: "Whoa, I'm impressed

with your diversity here, is this representative of your city council?"

Clearly it was not; so I think it makes sense. But, I think it's also important to have the right kind of candidate to make it happen. There may be people who aspire for it, who have aspired for it. But I think they don't get elected for various reasons: Another one is given the "Plan E" model we have here in the city—where we have a strong city manager and councilors elected at large across the entire city—it makes it hard for people in immigrant communities to get elected because there is no 'ward level' or neighborhood representation.

And also the time it takes.
It takes a lot of sacrifice and resources. All those factors discourage people from being engaged.

Did you ever endure any racism in the city and if so, what kind of experience did you have?
I can't say I experienced it lately. I think it's done in subtle ways, but to say that someone has come to my face and called me a derogatory name or something, I don't experience that here. To try to demean or belittle me blatantly, no. Does racism exist at the institutional level? Some people argue that it does and there's probably a good chance that it does, but it's very subtle. It's not right there in your face.

Do you also feel there's tension among different ethnic groups?
No, not at all, or not that I'm aware of anyway. I think by and large people are very friendly towards one another. There's not any one particular tension that exists. A lot of Africans go to Cambodian stores for their foodstuffs.

And a lot of Kenyans go to the Indian stores.
Exactly! I don't know how to say this without sounding ethnocentric, but I think by and large, Africans are very nice people. I think nice to a fault. Even though on the other hand, you look at it and you could say: "Well, wait a minute, why do they fight amongst themselves so much," looking at the instability that exists in a lot of the African countries. But I think towards foreigners, for the most part, people are very friendly in that sense.

Well, colonial border drawing caused a lot of the internal problems in Africa.
Yes, I didn't want to go there, but I do think that what we see going on in these

African countries is a result of that.

Is there one question you think I should have asked you, but didn't?
No, I think you really covered everything I expected you would want to cover. I can't think of any.

What about if you were doing this interview? Is there a question you might have asked that I did not?
Well, I think, and this might relate to your initial question, "How do I see myself and my future here in Lowell?"

So how do you see your future here in Greater Lowell?
I think the future is going to be rewarding. I think it is always hard to predict the future of course, but I think my overall goal is to really be of service to folks in Africa. I think that, yes, there are people in need here, but I think the need is not as great as in Sierra Leone. I don't know how I will be able to make such a transition. But that's something that I aspire for.

Do you think about going back to Sierra Leone, or would you like to do it through the United States?
My ideal scenario would be to work for an agency here and there like the U.S. Agency for International Development. This way I'm serving this country, and being of service over there, because I am a citizen of this country. And then there's the U.S. Department of Education, which is doing some international education initiatives to support literacy in some poor village or what-have-you…. A development project to bring electricity to people who don't have it… Clean water projects… I think that would be my ideal situation, so that I would be serving both the U.S. and people who need the help. So if you know of any job like that…!

Thanks for your time. I really appreciate it and I learned a lot.

CHAPTER SIX

Ivette Nieves

Ivette Nieves came to Lowell from Puerto Rico. She is a mother and grandmother. She works as a parent aide for Casey Family Services. Christoph Strobel and Yingchan Zhang interviewed Ivette on April 24, 2008.

> I have family all over the country, but I won't move out of Lowell! I have lived all over the city and I feel comfortable here. You help people, and people get to appreciate you. Even when I came here for the first time in 1992, I felt good, I felt comfortable, I am not afraid here. I feel comfortable living here. I don't want to leave; I want to stay here. Also my work, I love what I do, I love to work with people, and I think that's what makes me want to stay here.

I was raised in Puerto Rico. I came here when I was seventeen and finished my school here. I studied at Lowell High School.

What did you do after graduation?
I got training here and there. I went to Middlesex Community College. I did office work, manned the front desk, I was a nursing assistant, was employed as a teacher assistant… I did many things before I worked for House of Hope for eleven years as an associate manager.

So you work here now?
Yes I work at Casey Family Services —over seven years already! I came to Casey after I finished working at House of Hope. I have a good background working with people and families, that's my role here.

Can you give us a quick summary of what you do?
I'm a Parent Aide. I engage with families who need assistance. I help kids with school, their education, kids who are struggling with behavior at school. I go with their parents to school and help them out. Some of the parents, they have a lot of economic problems, and they don't necessarily know how to interact with the schools. I offer resources and can refer people to other places for more help. That's part of my job. I do a lot of outreach in the community. I engage a lot of people in groups, especially adults. I try to bring people out of their houses and get community participation.

What are some of the issues that you deal with in the schools?
Because we are the minority there are issues of racism and we also deal with a lot of peer pressure issues. It's difficult sometimes because some of the parents they don't have the language skills and they struggle to communicate with teachers and principals. They don't find support in school, or they don't know how to engage at the schools because of language barriers. It's part of my job to help parents to find a point person. I've been having problems in getting the support and keeping the support. Usually when you have a point person in school… there can be lay-offs due to lack of funding or grants. It is a struggle. I deal mostly with behavioral problems. I deal with kids who are in gangs and have issues with crime.

Do you mostly deal with Latino children or with children from all different backgrounds?
I'm more engaged in the Latino community because we have a particular lack of participation. I feel most comfortable doing that too. But I help everybody, whoever comes through this door.

Do you feel that there are better resources for, say, the Cambodian community as compared to the Latino community, or do you not see a difference there?
I don't see a difference. What I do feel though is that many Latinos will not engage in programs. This can be due to their immigration status. They don't want people to know that they don't have papers and they are here illegally, but also there is just a lack of information. Also grants that are funding programs are being cut.

You mentioned that when you work with kids you are also trying to figure out what their problems are, can you tell us a little bit about that?

I do an assessment. I meet with the parents first and I find out what their concerns are. Then from there I do a home visit. From there we set up an appointment to go to school and find out what the problem is. Then I put the pieces together: family, the kid's attitude, and I try to engage them in counseling groups here. You can usually figure out what is going on. The problems usually start at home. The parents don't speak English. The kids are born and raised here, they know the language, and they often don't know how to communicate with their parents. So I have to communicate with the parents. Kids often don't tell their parents about their academic performance or behavioral problems at school. It is a long process.

How many cases do you generally work on?
It goes up and down, and everybody is different. Some people they come to me for different reason. I have fifteen cases right now. It depends.

How would you describe your life in Lowell?
That is easy to answer. I just work and go home. [Laughter] I have family all over the country, but I won't move out of Lowell! I have lived all over the city and I feel comfortable here. You help people, and people get to appreciate you. Even when I came here for the first time in 1992, I felt good, I felt comfortable, I am not afraid here. I feel comfortable living here. I don't want to leave; I want to stay here. Also my work, I love what I do, I love to work with people, and I think that's what makes me want to stay here.

It sounds to me that your Latino identity is very important to you? Do you have a community here? Do you frequent Latino businesses such as restaurants and shops? Can you talk a little bit about that?
I would like to stay more active and engaged in the Latino community. I see more of it now than ever before. I see more restaurants opening up, little stores opening up, especially compared to fifteen years ago. I hope that there will be more growth, but I see some growth, and I think that is good. I know there are a lot of people who can do more, but too many things restrain us.

What kind of restraints? Is it the community? Is it the city or are there other factors?
I think it is us because we are still not strong enough. We still don't get together and get the word out. We say we are going to do this. We want to do this. We want to be heard. But we don't do it.

The numbers are there in the city. Is one issue maybe that Latino leadership has not emerged yet?
Exactly. We would need someone to push the issues and put the word out no matter what. Given the immigration status of many, there is fear. If you don't have the documentation, how are you going to represent yourself? I think that's part of it.

Do you feel that the Latino Community has increased in size since you arrived here?
I think it has stayed about the same.

Do you see an increase in Latino involvement in the city's activities?
I see some of it, but not as much as I would like to see. Casey Family Services runs Latino support groups, and we started with five people, and now we are fourteen. I see some growth, but not as much as I would like to see.

You mentioned that some people don't have legal documentation. What do you think keeps them here, even without the papers?
They just don't have the opportunity to fix their status. There are many people who came here illegally. They just get a fake Social Security with date of birth and they start working under the table and they feel comfortable with that. It's not much but at least they can support the people who they left behind in their country. They support their family. They don't come here to endanger anybody. They just came here to work. They just want to work and support their families because in their countries they don't have the same opportunities that we have here. After a while, they love it too much and they want to stay. But there is not much help out there to make the situation better, and the government is getting stricter and they get scared.

Do you feel that there is a crackdown? Because we talked to other people in the Latino community and they say that there are more ID checks.
It is not a crackdown it is an earthquake. It's terrible. Things that used to be so easily done before are now so difficult. Getting paperwork done now takes so much longer than it used to, and so many other things are so much more complicated.

What kind of activities do Latinos pursue to keep their identity strong?
We are trying our best to keep our customs. We have our parties and celebrations. That way we don't forget where we came from. But sometimes it is difficult because you get used to living here. As the years pass, you don't follow these things anymore.

It is really sad sometimes, to know that you lose things that you've grown up with.

What role does language play in your life? I assume you speak a lot of Spanish at work? Uh huh.

Do you have children?
I have four kids and I have a grandson too. Two came to the United States when they were babies, plus two were born here. All of them speak both languages. They speak English and Spanish in kind of a blurry way. Sometimes you don't understand what they say in Spanish. But they speak Spanish. No matter how much they complained how they didn't like to speak Spanish, when mommy came home they spoke Spanish. My grandson he is Cambodian and Puerto Rican. I love my baby grandson. He's going to speak three languages. I think it is really important for my kids to keep the language and use it a lot.

Do you find that there is pressure from mainstream society for your children not to learn Spanish? Do you find that the school is supportive or non-supportive on this issue? When I look at the United States, I'm always surprised how much it seems to be "English only." Do you experience that?
I noticed that when I came to United States. I felt the pressure to always speak English. I think that was one of the things that pushed me to go to school again. Try to get an education, try to learn the language, and try to be fluent. It was hard. Working at Casey, I saw a lot of families coming from various countries, speaking various languages; they had to struggle to adapt to the new language while not finding much support. It is difficult when the kids are trying and they don't find much support here. The language is crucial. You live here. You have to speak the language.

Do you feel that the schools are doing a good job in providing opportunities to foreign speakers to ease into English? Are there good programs to help with that?
The School Department, they offer good programs. But families have to be involved in their children's education too. Definitely you can find support, but it also depends on the parents and the kids. You want to go forward in life. You need good education. You have to apply yourself.

How did your children find school?

I never had those kinds of problems because my kids started school here. But I work with families whose children came here at age 12, 13, 14. The pressure is not even from the school—it is from their peers. If their parents are not involved, the kids just get lost. They end up in gangs, do crime, do whatever. Those children struggle a lot because they don't know the language.

Do you observe a lot of intergenerational issues between parents and kids?
Just imagine that parents come from Puerto Rico and they have never been to the United States. The kid comes from Puerto Rico and has never been to United States. Parents are trying to find support and can't find it. The kid won't find it either. So they're lost.

And those children will end up in gangs?
Exactly! Just to protect themselves. That's what they are looking for—protection. When they end up in gangs they get involved with crime. They skip school because they don't understand what is going on. So they just walk out of school. That's what I see.

Do a lot of people support relatives back home financially? You alluded to it earlier.
My guess would be seventy-five percent.

Wow! In what way does this play itself out?
Let me give you a specific example. A woman who came to the United States worked here for a couple of years. She got into a car accident and got benefits. She still supports her family with that benefit. She also goes to food pantries to collect food and clothes. She puts them in boxes and sends them to her family in her country. Because the income that she receives is not enough to support herself and her family, she collects things and sends packages. People work two or three shifts to send money home and to support themselves here. You see that a lot.

I noticed that the city has made some efforts to provide affordable housing. A large proportion of the Latino Community lives in public housing. What are the community's views on these issues?
I just left public housing two years ago. When I came to Massachusetts I was on welfare and with the little money that welfare gives you, you cannot pay regular rent. It was either that or move into a shelter. It's not easy to live on a low income. The rental

market rents are outrageous, and if you come here to work, to support people in your country, and support yourself here…! That's what many immigrants are looking for. They are looking for affordable housing. It is really difficult to get by. I think that's why the first thing many people do is look for affordable housing.

Do you find that those options are on the decline? Because a big discussion in the city now is that there is less affordable housing and there is gentrification going on. Do you see that in your work as well?

Prices are going up and up. It's crazy. People are looking for affordable housing. Nevertheless, the way housing is distributed should be a little more strategic. They should look into who exactly needs it. I know many people who don't need to live in public housing. They live better than me. [Laughs] They have four or five people in the family who work. They have a good enough income to pay market rate rent outside public housing and could leave the apartment to someone who really needs it. People should be conscientious too. There are people, they may need it for a couple of years, until they get on their feet, and they got better and they can go elsewhere.

That is my own experience. I was in Lowell [public] housing for eleven years. Now my kids are grown up. They are big. They work and they are out. I don't need to live in public housing because I can pay rent now. But I see families they don't move out; they raise their kids, and the kids end up living in housing to raise their kids, and they are still here. That's part of it. It is a cycle, and they just live on. They feel secure. They don't want to leave, because they don't want to try anything else.

Are you registered to vote?
Yes.

How about people in the community?
We do voter registration every year, before the primaries, for a whole week. We go around and ask people if they are already registered and we register people, a lot of them. It is important because we provide people with the right to vote. We have a lack of participation though. Many Latinos they don't have the privilege to vote because they are not citizens. We have a lot of people who are residents but they are not allowed to vote because they are not citizens yet. We also run voter education programs that teach people about the importance of voting, the reasons why they should vote, and to create awareness of the process.

You have a lot of Latinos, Southeast Asians, Africans, Indians, and so on in the city. But when you look at the city council, there is hardly any representation of people of color. How do you feel about that?

My dream is that a Latino person will go out and speak to all the Latinos in the community. That person will explain to them what voting means, the impact of their vote, and why it is important. I would like to see a friendly person when you go to city hall to help you find out how you can register in Spanish. I would also like more information available to immigrants in their native languages. I've been helping new voters for four or five years now, and I don't see any information. I have to really search for it. Maybe city hall, on voting day, could provide transportation to people who want to vote. Maybe that would be helpful to elderly people and adults who don't vote because they don't have transportation. I'd say we provide seventy percent of the transportation to the voting place.

Thank you so much for your time!

CHAPTER SEVEN

Anonymous 1 and 2

Anonymous 1 and Anonymous 2 are of Indian background. Like many immigrants from India in Lowell they hail from Gujarat. At the time of the interview, they both were nursing students at the University of Massachusetts Lowell. Christoph Strobel interviewed them on December 14, 2007.

My sophomore year of high school I started going to Lowell General Hospital for school related stuff. Then my grandmother went through a huge surgery. She had five by-pass surgeries that summer and I was already leaning towards nursing. So my family pushed me more into it, because they were all working. Summer, I had no school, so I spent a lot of time with my grandmother in Boston where she was in the hospital and that made me decide for sure.

—Anonymous 1

It was different for me because my dad went to college and then he didn't want to go. So he took over my grandfather's business. And my mom graduated high school and went one year [to college] and then she got married to my dad and then she just took over as a housewife and she never went back. And my dad at a young age just ran a business.

I feel like it was just different for me because I feel like I was the first to go to college and actually go through with it. I tell them that all the time, "My life is harder than yours if you believe it or not and I work and go to school and all that bit," but they tell me, "We had struggles too you know."

—Anonymous 2

I would like to know what section in Lowell you live in.
Anonymous 1: Oh, I live in Pawtucketville.

Great, and Anonymous 2?
Anonymous 2: I live in the Highlands.

Why did your families decide to move to the United States? Where did you live prior to your arrival in the U.S.? Did you make stops in between? Why don't we start out with Anonymous 1?
Anonymous 1: Why did we move to the U.S.? Better lifestyle. And then my other family had moved here too and they said, "Why don't you guys come?" So then my parents and my sister, they were the first ones to move here. When I was a year old they moved and went to Los Angeles because that is where my uncles were. So that's where they lived for about five, six years. And then from there we moved to Arizona; well my family moved to Arizona, and that's when I came, when I was about six years old, I don't remember. And we lived there for four years. From there we moved to Lowell.

Why did you come to Lowell?
Anonymous 1: Well, in Arizona we used to own a motel – our own business. But then my dad's brother, my other uncle who lived here, he was saying: "Why don't you try out just working." Because having your own business, it's hard. So my dad said, "Oh, ok, let's try something else." And we had family here.

So that drew you to Lowell. Who were you staying with before you were reunited with your parents? Were you staying with your grandmother?
Anonymous1: With my grandparents, yes. They were in India.

And was that in Gujarat or…?
Anonymous 1: Yes

Anonymous 2? What is your migration story please?
Anonymous 2: We came for a better lifestyle and better opportunities and my whole

family was also here. We were the last of the family from my dad's side to be in India. So, my dad's older sister, she filed for us to come here. We used to live in India too and my dad had his own business. He used to run my grandfather's business. So we all used to live together. And then they all moved here. And then we came.

Are you also from Gujarat?
Anonymous 2: Yes.

Did your family move to different parts of the United States before you came to Lowell, or did you end up straight here?
Anonymous 2: Just in Lowell.

What were your expectations, both of you, before you came to America? Did you have any preconceived notions about what it would be like?
Anonymous 1: I can't even remember what I was thinking. I was so young. But I remember when I came I was a little overwhelmed because you still expect it to be the same lifestyle. You don't know any better. It is a whole new environment. But then, as I started getting into it, I told myself: "Oh my gosh! This is totally different." And the language… I was in school in India. It was [in] English. I understood it and spoke a little. But it was still hard, going to school.

How about you?
Anonymous 2: I came here when I was twelve. I thought it would be like India. Everybody would be open and willing to welcome you. But it was different. There's the language barrier, obviously, because I understood English. But people didn't understand me, what I was trying to say to them. It was hard to make friends at school. It was difficult. But once you get used to it, it's fine.

How did you like the weather?
Anonymous 1: "Snow? What's snow?" It doesn't snow in India. Well, in some parts it does, but I had never seen it.

And then we have seven inches overnight! What advice would you give someone from the Indian community? Say someone shows up at the temple for the first time and they just moved to town. What advice would you give them about Lowell? Or anywhere else in the United States? What kind of advice do you wish someone gave you before you came to this country?

Anonymous 2: It's totally different. It's not what you expect. In India your friends are telling you, "Oh, you're going to America? It's going to be so much fun!"

Anonymous 1: They fantasize about it. But it's absolutely nothing like what you would hear in India. They tell you, "It's so nice," and, "You have no hardships." Blah, blah, blah. It's nothing like that. It's basically the same life. It's how you would live in India, except just a different environment.

How long have you lived in Lowell?
Anonymous 1: Nine to ten years.
Anonymous 2: Seven years.

Do you consider yourself as being part of the Highlands neighborhood or the Pawtucketville neighborhood? Does that not have an impact on your life?
Anonymous 2: I really don't consider it much.

Anonymous 1, where you live in Pawtucketville, are there a lot of Indians?
Anonymous 1: Oh, yes.

Anonymous 2, how about your area in the Highlands?
Anonymous 2: There are some but not as many as in Pawtucketville.

There seem to be a lot of Indians living in Middlesex Village?
Anonymous 2: But they are mostly South Indians?

Do you interact with those communities at all? Do you see them at temple or is that a different community altogether?
Anonymous 1: That is a different community all together. Not that we wouldn't interact with them. But we don't really see them. They have their own language, a different religion and culture.

Do they go to a different temple too? Or, do you know where their temple is?
Anonymous 2: They still come to ours.
Anonymous 1: During big festivals that every Hindu celebrates. They have their own temples. I don't think there's one around in Lowell.
Anonymous 2: No, there is one in the Framingham area—Lakshmi Temple.

Is there a difference between the types of Hinduism they practice and the Hinduism you practice?

Anonymous 1: It's just small beliefs that we have, like Protestants and Catholics. There are so many parts to it.

Anonymous 2: Certain Hindus would celebrate some festivals differently than others. They consider certain festivals important and we would consider others. One big one is our Indian New Year, Diwali. That's common.

I know when we came to the temple a while back there was a lot of food being served, very good food by the way, is that happening during the New Year as well?

Anonymous 1: Oh yes. Well, during Diwali, we just went, it was in November. It's a four-day, five night event, but at the temple it's usually three or four days. From Thursday, Friday, Saturday, Sunday.

Anonymous 2: One day we worship for our prosperity. We thank god for that and for helping us to be prosperous all year long. On Saturday we celebrate the actual New Year. We have many food items that we offer to god.

Anonymous 1: It's like a mountain of food displayed in front of the deity. It's usually all different types of food and people make it. So whoever, whatever they want to make they bring it in. It gets offered to god.

Your temple is a key part of your community life. Are there any stores you go to as well? Or restaurants that you like to go to?

Anonymous 1: Well the Indian stores, there are three stores, one in Pawtucketville, one in the Highlands and one on Middlesex street.

Do you go to other places to shop for clothing, if you're looking for more traditional saris or can you get them...

Anonymous 1: Well, a lot of people do shop here, but I know both of our families, we don't shop here. Our families go to India every couple of years. We just shop there. And there's always stuff online.

That's the Internet. That's globalization. But for food items do you shop at the Indian stores? Or do you go mostly to Market Basket or Hannaford's or those kinds of supermarkets?

Anonymous 2: It's kind of mixed. It's not like we just shop at the Indian store or just at Market Basket. If we need something like Indian flour or something, we go to the Indian store, but if we need vegetables or something we go to Market Basket for example.

Are there any particular vegetables or food items you can only get at the Indian store? I've been to the Indian stores and they sell some really neat stuff. But do you feel that the supermarkets and businesses in town cater to your tastes as well?

Anonymous1: I do feel Indian stores have more specific stuff. You get more and it's cheaper. Market Basket and Hannaford's might package it and carry it, but their packaged stuff is less and more expensive.

You've mentioned that your family goes back to India at least every now and then. Can you talk a little bit more specifically about why you go, probably to visit family, but how often that is, how you travel?

Anonymous 1: Well okay, since I've been here, I've been to India twice, and a lot of times my family goes back because of family stuff. My cousin's wedding. Even though they live in the U.S., it just feels better if you have an Indian wedding in India because you have all the traditional stuff and everything. That's why I've been back. Once for my cousin's wedding and once for my sister's wedding even though they were both here. The family goes down there, and my sister went down there again for her sister-in-law's wedding. It comes around like that, weddings, other family stuff, just to visit.

Is there any other place you travel to see family?

Anonymous 1: In India we have family all over the place, in different cities in Gujarat. So we visit them. I don't know if you remember, last year we talked about that religious monument that was built there. We went last time to visit there. We went to see the Taj Mahal. It depends on the time, because when you go there, you feel like you don't have enough time. It's usually for three weeks or something like that.

And you also have family obligations?

Anonymous 1: Yes.

And if you don't visit they get mad?

Anonymous 1: Exactly.

How about you?

Anonymous 2: I actually haven't been back since I've been here. My mom went just in January. She was saying that it takes a lot of time to mostly visit the family, but one reason she went was to visit my grandparents. If I would go, I feel like it would be so different.

Anonymous 1: It is different. The first time I went it was five years after I'd been here and then I went three years later on, and I was like, "Oh my gosh, I was just here," but it's so different.

Do you miss not being able to go back?
Anonymous 2: Yes. Plus all of my friends have been back since I've been here and they tell me: "Oh, it's this, this..." and I haven't even been back.

I understand. Have you traveled outside Lowell much?
Anonymous 2: Well just this past summer we were in Canada, New Jersey, and Florida.

And that was all in connection with the temple? So what happened last summer? We talked about it at the temple? You got an important visitor, right?
Anonymous 1: This year is extra special, because it is the hundred-year celebration for our organization. The successor of our organization came and toured North America. We went to every place with him.

So people traveled throughout North America to spend as much time with the leader as they could?
Anonymous 1: A lot of people from our temple did. This weekend is the big celebration of the hundred-year anniversary.

You both go to school here at UMass Lowell in the Nursing Program, right?
Anonymous 1 and Anonymous 2: Yes.

Do you work outside of school? Or are you just able to focus on school?
Anonymous 1: I worked my freshman year at Lowell General Hospital and now I just work in the School of Health and Environment.

Is that a work-study position?
Anonymous 1: Yes.
Anonymous 2: I actually work at Market Basket. It's different.

Do you like it?
Anonymous 2: Sometimes it gets hard to balance school and work. But I'm used to it.

How many hours do you work?
Anonymous 2: I usually work twenty hours a week.

That's a lot.
Anonymous 1: I don't get much in. Probably about five hours with the work study.

Are you able to balance your work and your class work?
Anonymous 2: Most of those nineteen hours come from the weekend. I usually work ten hours on Saturday and probably six or seven on Sundays. I usually don't work much on weekdays.

Do you eat at some of the local restaurants too or do you just eat at home?
Anonymous 1: Indian restaurants?

Indian restaurants or maybe you like going to other restaurants?
Anonymous 1: We eat out a lot together. But we don't go to Indian restaurants a lot.
Anonymous 2: We usually go to the Cheesecake Factory or places like that.
Anonymous 1: I recently went to the Indian restaurant on Middlesex Street. It's really good. I went with my cousins. They go there all the time and like to order out there.

Are your parents more traditional about their eating choices?
Anonymous 1: They eat everything.
Anonymous 2: Yeah, they eat everything.
Anonymous 1: They like Italian and Mexican.

Does your family have a garden to grow vegetables or do they have no time to do that? Or is there no land to do that?
Anonymous 1: We don't have a garden, but my mom and dad usually have pots where they grow some bell peppers. That's what they did this summer. They usually grow tomatoes, stuff like that. They like doing that especially when my grandmother is around.

So they do it on the balcony of their apartment?
Anonymous 1: Yeah.
Anonymous 2: When we moved here we used to live with my uncle in Framingham and he used to do the whole bit. The whole bell peppers and tomatoes, but I don't like gardening.

Do you feel that your family does it because it reminds them of home?
Anonymous 2: It just gives them something to do. It keeps them busy.

How would you describe, we already alluded to it a little bit, how do you think life is different from India? I've heard two strains, that it's not very different and that it's very different. How do you think life in Lowell compares to life back home in India? Or I should ask you both, which seems more home now? Is Gujarat more your home? Or Lowell? Or both?

Anonymous 1: I'd say both. Gujarat is my background. That's where I grew up and that's where I'm from. And Lowell is home. When I go to India after a while it's time to come back, and it's like home, ahhh.

How about you?

Anonymous 2: I lived longer in India than here. But I still consider Lowell as my home. Gujarat is where we come from.

Do your parents feel different about that, or do you not talk to your parents about that?

Anonymous 1: No, I think it's the same with them. I know my parents when we are over they feel that it's time to go back, especially my mom.

Anonymous 2: Yeah, my mom, she would call us from India and she would tell us: "I miss you guys so much. I want to come back right now."

Do you find life different between the two places and what specifically strikes you as different between the two places? And what do you feel is really similar?

Anonymous 1: Well, what I always talk about with my parents is how much more independent we are here, especially after coming from India. In India you're just dependent on your parents. Here, everybody says, "I need to get a job," or "I get to have a job," people get excited about it. But in India you solely focus on school and then after school you go on to work and stuff like that, but until then you're basically dependent on your parents.

Anonymous 2: That's one major difference. Responsibility here hits you early. You learn to take care of yourself at an early age while in India everyone depends on his or her parents. You wouldn't want to be by yourself. You wouldn't want to go get a job.

The perception about America is that it's a very individualistic country? Do you feel that's having an impact on the way Indian families now live in Lowell?

Anonymous 1: Well, the whole community is definitely more individualistic. In India everyone is always there. I feel like you're always connected, while here… I'll give you an example. If I haven't been to the temple for three weeks. I don't know what's going on with other people. In India you would see them on the streets.

Anonymous 2: Moms go down and cut vegetables together. Kids play outside.

Anonymous 1: Yeah—but here, everybody has to work and then you come home in the evening and you just want to watch television or sleep.

Do you feel people have to work more here than back in India or is that not a fair observation?

Anonymous 1: I wouldn't say they have to work more, but they think they have to work more. Here, life is based on working. While in India everybody says, "Oh yeah, I have to go to work." But it's not an eight-hour shift or a twelve-hour shift. It's starting to become more like that now in India too though.

Why do you think that is? Globalization?

Anonymous1: Yeah.

We already talked a little bit about your relationship with your parents. You seem to have a pretty good relationship with your parents. Do you feel that there are sometimes frictions about certain issues, or do you talk things through?

Anonymous 2: I feel with me going out on certain occasions, they tell me, "No you can't go," but then I'll tell them, "I haven't been out in four months." And they'll say, "It seems like you've been going out every weekend," or something like that. It's small stuff, not huge issues.

Anonymous 1: I feel like I'm able to talk to my parents. But sometimes growing up, there were frictions about silly stuff, but other than that, no big issues.

You just mentioned your sister got married. Did she get married to a person she met in Lowell?

Anonymous 1: No, no, no, she met him in India the first time she went. They both came back and then they went back to get married.

But now they live in the United States?

Anonymous 1: They live in Lowell.

You mentioned the wedding. The little I know about India is that weddings are a very big deal. Can you talk a little bit about what happened at your sister's wedding?

Anonymous 2: She could go on for hours probably.

Anonymous 1: First of all it was a five-day event. So the first day is when family first starts coming in, just different family from India. And then the second day, do you know about henna? So, there's a ceremony for that when the ladies just get together and everybody gets that done on their hands. The third night was basically a dance night. But it's Indian traditional dancing. Everybody just gets together from the brides side and the groom's side, and they have food there. The fourth day is when everything starts coming together.

They have a ceremony at the bride's place separate from the one going on at the groom's place. And then on the fifth day is the real wedding. But it was really big because in my family we have all men and my sister and me are the only women, and she was the first one to get married.

Is there a traditional way to divide up the wedding costs? Where I come from, traditionally, it's always the parents of the bride who have to pay for everything. Is it the same in India? Or are the costs being split?
Anonymous 1: It used to be that the woman's side had to pay for everything. But now the costs are often split. But the wedding part, you know how I said it's a five-day event, but the wedding, the main day; I still think it's taken care of mostly by the bride's family. I don't know about your culture, but in India, the wedding happens where the bride is, where her family is, or her city, hometown. So the groom has to travel with his family and everybody comes.

The five-day ceremonies do they often occur in a different city or in different parts of the country?
Anonymous 1: Yep. And everything doesn't have to happen in five days, but I think that is the tradition. Nowadays people change and want to do things their way too.

How does your family stay connected? Do you talk by phone? E-mail?
Anonymous 2: We just talked to my grandparents the other day and we usually call them every other week to see how they're doing.

Is your family thinking of maybe bringing your grandparents to the U.S.?
Anonymous 2: Well my mom's brother, and my mom's sister, they live in England and my grandparents could have stayed there; but they didn't like it there.

Did you visit your family in England at all?
Anonymous 2: Actually two of my cousins came here a couple years ago, but I haven't had a chance.

Do you have family visiting you from India at all, like your grandparents?
Anonymous 2: They don't like to travel.

What about you? Do you phone?
Anonymous 1: A lot of my family is here from both sides. But my dad's older brother, he has two brothers, the middle one, his whole family is in India. They don't want to come here. We usually call them. My grandparents, they're getting older, so we call them more often. I stay in touch with my cousins by email.

You've always been in touch with your cousins through email? Or was there a shift where you used to write letters and then switched over to email?
Anonymous 1: Not always. When I was younger I used to just talk to them on the phone, but then when I could get on the computer myself I started to e-mail.
Anonymous 2: It was different for me. When I moved here I didn't know about e-mail and I used to write my friends letters and they used to write me, but now it is e-mail.
Anonymous 1: If I could add to that. Over time, I have lost touch with my cousins. I'm not as close to them as I used to be. I used to be really close to them when we were there. But now I feel like we've grown apart. I mean I still talk to them because they're my cousins.

Were you living close to them when you lived in India?
Anonymous 1: Yeah.

So it is kind of like childhood friends that you have outgrown?
Anonymous 1: And they were all boys too.

Do you feel that your life is different from that of your parents?
Anonymous 2: Totally.
Anonymous 1: I wouldn't say totally from my parents because I talk to them all the time about it and tell them that my life is so much harder than theirs. They don't understand. But when they talk to me I don't think it's totally different.

They grew up in India. They both went to college. And I know my dad had to work while he was in college and he went away too, so he had to cook his own food and stuff at that time. That was a big deal especially in India. In America people go to college all the time. So I don't think it's that different. But they did it in India and not here, and everything here is so much harder, it takes so much more to graduate.

Do you feel like your parents are pushing you to get educated because they have college education and they see a value in it?

Anonymous 1: I don't feel like they've ever had to push me. You have to do it.

Anonymous 2: We push ourselves.

Anonymous 1: Yes, we push ourselves.

Anonymous 2: We have to do it.

Anonymous 1: Yes, we see value in it.

Obviously you feel like you have to do it. But is it because you feel like you owe it to your parents to do well?

Anonymous 2: Yes.

Anonymous 1: Exactly. And when I was in India, I remember as a kid I didn't want to go to school, but my cousins pushed me more. They would be like you have to do well, this is good. And if I did a little bad they would ask me why did you do badly on it? So I feel like this is the way I was brought up and so now I push myself.

Anonymous 2: It was different for me because my dad went to college and then he didn't want to go. So he took over my grandfather's business. And my mom graduated high school and went one year [to college] and then she got married to my dad and then she just took over as a housewife and she never went back. And my dad at a young age just ran a business.

I feel like it was just different for me because I feel like I was the first to go to college and actually go through with it. I tell them that all the time, "My life is harder than yours if you believe it or not and I work and go to school and all that bit," but they tell me, "We had struggles too you know."

Is there anything that you hope if you have children some time yourself, that you feel you would like to pass on to your children? That you would think is very important for your family's past background and being Indian-Americans? Does that question make sense?

Anonymous 1: We always talk about that. We want them to know the language, Gujarati, and we want to pass down traditions, basic Indian traditions.

Anonymous 2: Like attend temple and stick to their roots you know.

Do you feel that you're getting similar encouragement from your parents to do that?

Anonymous1 and Anonymous 2: Yes.

Is there a Gujarati school attached to the temple? I know you both speak Gujarati. But

is there an infrastructure to help language learners?
Anonymous 1: At the temple, there are volunteers. They teach the younger kids how to write Gujarati and to read. That's what we speak at the temple. That's how kids grow up, and many speak it at home too.

Do you feel this is changing with the next generation?
Anonymous 1: Definitely, especially with my brother. He was born here. It took him a while to get the language down. When he was younger he used to say stuff and people would wonder what he was trying to say. We made fun of him all of the time. He's picking it up. But it depends on your family and how you're brought up. If my brother hadn't been brought up this way he wouldn't have spoken Gujarati. But with my parents, and having my sister and me always talking to him, it's helped him.

Do you have examples of that too?
Anonymous 2: I talk to my sister all the time. But sometimes she forgets some words because she's learning English. And I tend to yell at her, "How do you forget, you've been speaking this all your life?"
Anonymous 1: And it goes on with my cousins—the ones who were born here. It's funny. They speak better Gujarati than I do. But that has to do with how their parents raised them.

For a lot of immigrant families there's an expectation from folks back home that they also support the family back home. Maybe this is a question that your parents would be better at answering, but do you have to support family in India as well, or is your family back in India economically self sufficient?
Anonymous 1: A lot of my family is already here. I think my uncle and other distant family, they take care of themselves. If they were to ever need help my parents would.
Anonymous 2: My dad's family is here. But on my mom's side, my mom's brother from England, he sends money to my grandparents because they're too old to work. So he gets their house repaired and sends them money.

Your temple is very active when there are national catastrophes.
Anonymous 1: They do it not just in India, but also all over the world. Here during Hurricane Katrina, but also during the tsunami, the earthquakes that happened in Gujarat, flood relief. It's all over the world, not just India.

Does your organization support or operate businesses or schools that you therefore support?
Anonymous1: They have hospitals in India and schools.

You both are training to become nurses. Did you always want to do that?
Anonymous1: My mind has changed a couple of times growing up. In middle school, until my sophomore year in high school, I wanted to be a lawyer because I thought I was so good at arguments I could win. Like with my parents, my cousin or my sister I would say, "I'm going to be a lawyer, I can win at anything." I'm good at convincing, that's what my cousins say. And then I wanted to be an engineer; that lasted for six months.

My sophomore year of high school I started going to Lowell General Hospital for school related stuff. Then my grandmother went through a huge surgery. She had five by-pass surgeries that summer and I was already leaning towards nursing. So my family pushed me more into it, because they were all working. Summer, I had no school, so I spent a lot of time with my grandmother in Boston where she was in the hospital and that made me decide for sure.

How about you?
Anonymous 2: I changed so many times. When I was little my parents would ask me what I wanted to be when I grew up and I would say a doctor. But when I came here and realized a doctor has twelve years of school, I don't think I could handle that much school. And I also like to interact with patients.

I volunteered at Lowell General for two years over the summer and I saw how the nurses worked with patients. Probably in high school I thought of becoming a nurse.

What's your favorite Indian celebration? Is it the New Year?
Anonymous1 and Anonymous 2: Yes.
Anonymous 1: Everybody is so happy to see each other. It's the one time you see everyone.
Anonymous 2: You see everybody.
Anonymous1: That's when we talk to everybody, even distant relatives.
Anonymous 1: Diwali is the Festival of Lights and it's all about family, basically like Christmas. People give gifts.

Do you celebrate Christmas too or not at all?
Anonymous1: Well, I think over the years we've grown out of it. I know with my

brother we always used to do Christmas. But the past couple of years we haven't. But I like the whole idea of Christmas, because people are so happy and I like it when people are excited. It's something different from everyday life.

Do you have relatives come to Lowell or people from your organization and if so, do you take them to any specific places, like your temple or anything touristy?
Anonymous 1: My cousins came over one year from California and then my uncle and my aunt, my mother's brother were over last summer. We went to Boston, showed them around the temple, visiting other relatives we have around here, that's basically it.

Do you feel like you get discriminated against for being Indian? Or that you're thrown in with different types of immigrant groups when you're in town, or may-be when you were in high school?
Anonymous 2: For me it was in middle school when I moved here.
Anonymous 1: I think it's changed. The community is growing especially at Lowell High. Not just the Indian community. There are many other communities. There are always going to be stereotypes about people; what are you going to do about it?

So in middle school people made fun of you?
Anonymous 2: They would pick on me. I don't know why, because I'm Indian or because I just came here. I never knew the reason.
Anonymous 1: I think for her it might have been the age of the kids. Because when I came here in second or third grade, I remember the kids were helpful.
Anonymous 2: For my sister, because she was younger, she was only in second grade; she wasn't having as hard a time. High school was totally different I would say.

Middle school is the meanest time.
Anonymous 1: It is! Even for me! I was here and I remember kids picking on other kids and thinking: "Oh my gosh, that is so mean!"

Do you feel that there are tensions within the Indian communities in Lowell or between the Indian communities and other communities? Or is that not part of your experience?
Anonymous 2: I don't know of anything to be honest.
Anonymous 1: There might be some things that could raise tensions, but I don't know of anything.

Do you care about politics? Do you know much about politics in the city?
Anonymous 2: No, I don't.
Anonymous 1: I used to when I was going through middle school, high school. I guess I used to be more in tune to it during the debates. But now I have no time. My dad is into it. He always tells me stuff.

Is he into international politics or local politics?
Anonymous 1: Both.

One thing that comes up and that people raise as an issue in the immigrant communities is they would like to see more immigrants on the city council. In other words, there are Irish Americans and French Canadians on the council. But there's a lot of Cambodians in the city and no Cambodian representation on the city council. Are you concerned about that? Would you like to see an Indian on the city council, or do you feel like the city is taking care of your community?
Anonymous 1: I'm trying to think more about what my parents would think because right now I have no opinion. My dad, when he sees other cities or other parts of America and sees an Indian council person, he would probably say, "Hey, look it's an Indian." But I don't hear complaints from them. Niki Tsongas [Congresswoman representing Lowell] came over when we did the walk-a-thon, so they're involved in our community. At the walk-a-thon, which we do annually, there's always one guest from the city.

How do you feel about the educational opportunities, obviously you've gone through middle school, high school and college all in the city of Lowell. Do you feel like you're getting a good education in the city? Are there things that could be improved?
Anonymous 1: I think they do a god job with education and providing opportunities for everybody.
Anonymous 2: No complaints.

Do you think that Lowell has changed since you got here?
Anonymous 1: The one thing that I think has changed is the downtown area. When we used to go Lowell High School, we'd have to go downtown to catch the buses and it was unsafe. I used to rush out of school, so that I could get the early bus and not have to go to downtown. But I think it's changed a lot now. My brother goes to Lowell High and they don't have to go to downtown. I think they made that safer for the kids.

I understand too that downtown has gotten a lot safer.
Anonymous 2: Cops are out and people. One time I had to be there at night and I was really scared, but I feel like it's getting safer, it's getting there.

Are you thinking about leaving Lowell at some point? Would you like to live in the city or will it depend on jobs and careers?
Anonymous 1 and Anonymous 2: Jobs.

What about your parents? Are they going to stay in Lowell?
Anonymous 1: They always talk about moving but we'll see what my dad thinks.

Are your parents thinking about moving to Gujarat at some point? Retiring there or do they want to stay in the U.S.?
Anonymous 2: When my parents moved here, they said, "We'll get you married and through school and then you can take care of your sister and we'll move back and retire there," but I doubt they'll go back.
Anonymous 1: My dad always says that too.

Once you start to have children and their grandchildren are here, they're probably not going to go back.

If there's one thing you could change in your experience as an immigrant in Lowell, what would it be?
Anonymous 1: I really can't think of anything because I always compare it with how it would have been if I were still living in Arizona. Lowell is so different from there. Where I lived was such a small town and there were a lot of Indians there too, but not as many as here and you'd see the Indians and it would be the Indians and a bunch of white people. Here it's open. There are so many different communities it's just like a little world in itself. There wasn't much to do for us [in Arizona].
Anonymous 2: I have a friend who moved from Lowell to Kansas and she definitely misses Lowell. She never expected to miss it as much. Lowell is so alive. There's so much to do.
Anonymous 1: You have your freedom here, there so much community everyone is used to seeing all the different cultures.

CHAPTER EIGHT

Francisco Carvalho

Francisco Carvalho, an immigrant from Brazil, came to Lowell in the late 1960s. A community activist and worker for many years, he is a father and a husband and after a long career in banking, he is the Executive Director of Mill Cities Community Investments. Christoph Strobel interviewed him on January 23, 2008.

> I am an American and proud to be an American. When I became a citizen, I did not become a citizen because this country had a lot to give me. I felt at that time that I needed to become a citizen because I had so much to give to the country. That's what I tried to do. But you can't forget who you are. Because then all the qualities that made you go away. I am Brazilian. I got my foundation; I got everything that I believe in when I was in Brazil. I remember being ten, eleven years old and I was fascinated by the Kennedys and cried when John Kennedy got assassinated.

My name is Francisco J. Carvalho, I'm originally from Brazil, and presently live in Tyngsboro.

You did live in Lowell before though?
Yes, when I came to the United States in 1969 I lived in Lowell on Black Brook Drive and then in 1971 I moved to the Back Central area. In 1974 I moved near UMass Lowell in the north canal area and that was my last address in Lowell. I bought a house in Tyngsboro and have been there ever since.

Why did you decide to move to the United States?

It was not my decision. I was fifteen years old and my father had passed away in 1968. With his passing, there was a lot of financial hardship because he had cancer. Cancer treatment at that time in Brazil was very expensive. At the same time, I had three brothers who played professional soccer in Boston, with the Boston Astros from the old American soccer league, and the team was based in Lowell. Due to a lot of pressure from my father's family in Brazil, we could not go to school and get a job. So the older brothers thought it would be better to get away from the pressure of the family. My mother decided to sell everything we had, and we immigrated to the United States in 1969. November 11th was finally when we put our foot in Lowell and three days after that I saw my first snowflakes. And while it was exciting at first, it soon became old news.

Did you have any preconceptions about what life was going to be like before you moved to America?
The impression you get from watching the movies and following things through the news and TV at the time was completely different from what I found. I found that the housing was made out of less sturdy material as opposed to bricks, which we had in Brazil. You had to be careful how you touched the walls. Housing, the apartments side by side, those were things I wasn't really expecting.

I was expecting, I don't know, a country where houses were beautiful. I also thought the people were going to be very cold people, and to a certain extent, at the beginning, without speaking much English, it was not a very 'warm climate'. As a matter of fact, I remember getting a job at a fast food place two months after I got here. It was the middle of winter, and my boss, because I couldn't speak English would give me the hose and tell me to go wash the parking lot and then yell at me because it turned into ice, and things like that. So I said these people have a weird sense of humor. Over the years I was able to realize that there were opportunities here that I would never have had in Brazil.

Did you come here by plane or by boat?
We came by plane. It was the longest trip. It was a Peruvian airline that left Rio and went to Peru. From Peru we stopped in Panama. From Panama we stopped in New York. From New York we went to Boston. It took forever.

So did you come directly to Lowell or did you move around a little bit at first?
We came directly to Lowell

Do you still work in Lowell?
Yes, since I got here I have worked within a mile of each place. I went from working at a pizza place downtown to Beneficial Finance right down the street. Then I went to a bank up the street and then I went to Enterprise Bank, less than a mile away. I left to go work for the Coalition for a Better Acre, which was about a mile away also. Presently I work on Gorham Street, which is near the Portuguese area. And I own the pizza place where I used to work in the early 1970s, Espresso Pizza. I've co-owned it with my brothers for nineteen years.

Do you get a lot of customers who are Portuguese speakers?
We do at the bank because that was part of the bank's mission. The owner of the bank grew up in Back Central. So he wanted to give something back to the community. That's why he put a branch there. In my branch we speak Portuguese on a daily basis.

You lived in Back Central and now you work there. Do you consider yourself part of that neighborhood?
Let me go back a few steps. In 1969, 1970, when I first moved to the United States, I used to live on Black Brook Drive. I met the woman who is now my wife and who grew up in the Back Central area. She was born there and she grew up there. I got married at St. Anthony's Church and until sixteen or eighteen months ago I had been associated with the church as the treasurer. I went back to school to get a master's degree. Running a business and working at the bank, I didn't have time to do that anymore. So I resigned. I have really never left Back Central. My kids went to church there. I played soccer at the Portuguese club, both Portuguese clubs. I played in both of them, until recently when I put on weight. So I have been always connected to the community.

Most recently the Catholic Church was having some turmoil and wanted to close some churches. They wanted to combine the Portuguese church with others, and I was one of five people who led the charge for that not to happen. I'm entrenched in that part of the city. I participated in neighborhood group meetings, and I still go on occasion to keep in touch with what's going on there. So yes, I'm very much involved with that section of Lowell.

Is it the same sort of neighborhood than it was?
It's a completely different neighborhood from what it used to be when I was growing

up. It was predominately Portuguese. With the passage of time and the Portuguese immigration stopping in the 1970s, and as part of the process of Portuguese immigrants making a success of their lives here, they became a little bit more affluent, and they began to buy homes in the suburbs and started to move. They would still own some of the properties as rentals, but they were moving to the suburbs. They still came back for church, the festivals, and to the clubs, but as far as living there...

You now have a very big Brazilian contingent which has moved in, and which is completely different. I always say that although we speak the same language and were colonized by the Portuguese, there is an ocean between us. And that ocean is also present in day-to-day life. Besides the Brazilians, there are a lot of Cambodians who have moved into the area along with the Hispanics, so the makeup of the community has changed.

Do you feel that there are tensions between the Brazilians and the Portuguese because of the "ocean"? How's the relationship?
It's much better now than back in the early 1970s. Back at that time, the Brazilians who were here were here in smaller numbers and the Brazilians did not respect the Portuguese as they should have been respected. Mainly because a lot of the Brazilians that were here had some formal education, while the Portuguese were mostly farmers and fishermen from the different island. That created some tension.

And, some Brazilians rather than families like mine, were coming by themselves, and lived in housing that was owned by Portuguese. They started to owe some money and take off and not pay. That created a lot of bad feeling with the Portuguese towards the Brazilians. The last ten years or so, there was a change in that more and more Brazilian families have started moving into the area rather than the individual single guys or ladies.

There seemed to be more stability in the community and some nice friendships emerged. Is it to the point where all the differences are aside? No. As recently as three, four years ago, when we tried to see if the Brazilian church and the Portuguese church could combine under one roof, there was resistance on both sides.

You mentioned that the Brazilians that came were better educated than the Portuguese?
Well, at least they thought so!

Do you think that it is the same today?

The Brazilians who are here did not really have the opportunity to follow their professions. You have a lot of Brazilians who came and were farmers themselves or worked doing manual labor and so forth. But you find a lot of Brazilians who are teachers, bankers, attorneys, who did not have the economic opportunities to follow their careers in Brazil. The Brazilian community is a mixture. I found at the bank sometimes, there are still some Portuguese who sign with an "X." Others are very sophisticated.

I think due to the larger numbers you still have a good amount of people who are well educated, but you do have a very high percentage who only have minimal education who come from Brazil; maybe that leveled the playing field a little bit.

Do you differentiate between Portuguese and Brazilian businesses or does that matter to you?

To me as a person, it does not. The Portuguese community adopted me a long time ago. I have the utmost respect for the Portuguese. My wife is Portuguese. My kids are half Brazilian, half Portuguese. I have the most respect for both cultures. But when it comes to business, there is a major difference. The Portuguese community is more stable. They have been here longer. They don't have the same issues as the Brazilian community does.

In the Brazilian community a lot of the members who are here have overstayed their visas and therefore they don't have the credentials to deal with a formal organization like a bank. The services I can provide to the Brazilian community are limited. There are a number of Brazilian merchants and business people who have their situation all taken care of and therefore we can do business and offer them a vast array of services. But a vast majority of them are not in that situation so it's different. It's difficult.

Do you frequent Brazilian and Portuguese businesses in the Back Central area?

I love eating, so I'm either at a Brazilian store or restaurant a couple times a week or I'm at a Portuguese store or restaurant a couple times a week.

What are your favorite restaurants?

I like Rios and I like the Portuguese clubs. You can't beat the Portuguese clubs as far as the food they put out, the price, and the atmosphere. I'm a member of them.

I've heard good things about them. Are they open for members only?

No they are open to the general public.

Do you still have a lot of friends in Lowell or has that changed with suburbanization?
I go to Tyngsboro to sleep every night. For the last 37 years of my life Lowell has been my home. As a matter of fact, when people ask me where I am from when I travel, I say Lowell. Tyngsboro is where I go to sleep at night and where my family is. When I'm off working at the pizzeria or the bank, Lowell is really what I consider my hometown. I grew up in Lowell. I have done a lot of work to improve the quality of life in Lowell, both through the bank and also as an executive director of a community development corporation [Coalition for a Better Acre]. So that's where I've spent most of my time. My friends, most of them, are in Lowell, and they range from Brazilians, to Portuguese, to Africans, and Americans, so it's a wide range.

Do you get to go back to Brazil?
I've been to Portugal. I went to the Azores in 1978 when I went there to play soccer with my Portuguese team. I have not been back to Brazil since 1972. I'm hoping to graduate from my studies in May and my gift to myself for graduation is going to be a trip to Brazil. I'm working on getting my paperwork all set so I can spend two or three weeks in Brazil during the summer.

Are you going to take your family?
Yes, if they want to come. But I won't force them. My youngest daughter is dying to go. My wife feels she doesn't know if she wants to be on a plane for nine hours, but we'll work things out. In the end, I think most of them will come.

Let's talk about family a little bit. You met your wife in Lowell and she is Portuguese and you have at least two daughters…
Two daughters and one son. The youngest one is 20, my son is 21 and my oldest will be 23 on January 30th. I think the influence of family for me goes back to how I grew up. I have the utmost respect for my mother; she left her country, her friends, everything that she owned to make sure that her kids had a better life. We came to a strange country, different language, different customs, when she was 56 years old. She had a good life. She was here for about 28 years before she passed away. She learned a little bit of English. She was an inspiration to us.

Very early on, my brothers and I made a decision. Right now I have four living brothers and a sister. One of my brothers passed away about three, four years ago.

But we made a decision we would try to honor what we learned in Brazil. What that meant is that we would take care of my mother when she got old. So we kept my mother from the nursing home. We made her a promise and we honored our word. She was home until the very end, when she needed some medical attention, and then the doctor said she needed to go to a place for rehab before she could go home. She never came back because of her health issues.

But she was somebody that everything revolved around, Christmas, holidays, everything was around her. It happens the same way with my family. We have our get-togethers, mostly during the holidays, so family was something instilled in me as I was growing up and it remains with me to this day.

What are your aspirations for your children?
I have worked all my life to provide them with the resources and everything that they need to be good citizens, to be good people, down to earth, and to this date, things are working out as planned. My kids went to private school to get the best education that I could buy them. The number one reason I have not gone back to Brazil is because I invested in my kid's education rather than vacations. I went almost twenty years without taking a vacation because I've got a mortgage to pay, three tuitions to pay for. We made a decision that my wife would not work outside the home to be there for the kids, which is unusual today.

All those things were decisions that were made because I wanted to give my kids a chance to succeed and provide them with as much stability and support at home as possible. It's all about choices and that's the choice that we made. So, I'm very happy to report that my kids are hard working, they're down to earth when people meet them, they aren't bragging about different things. I like my kids. I like spending time with them and doing things with them. They don't mind me going to the mall with them or things like that, which nowadays is a big thing. Most kids don't like that. We went camping for a while and I would go dance with them and what teenager wants to be seen with their parents, right? We have a strong sense of family where we try to look out for each other and help each other.

Do you still have contact with either your extended family in the Azores or in Brazil?
I don't have contact with my extended family. I do have my immediate family, my brothers and sister and one of my brothers is my partner in the pizza business so we're in daily contact. We have a lot of Brazilian friends, either through soccer or

something else that we are in daily contact with. I got a call the other day, it was a promotion from one of the Brazilian businesses and my prize was getting unlimited calls to Brazil for a month, and I asked her if she could give me a list of people to call so I could use my prize! When I told her I had not been back in thirty-five years she was amazed by it.

Do you speak Portuguese at home?
Not at home, my kids unfortunately, I was always working and my wife speaks mostly English so they always spoke English. I only speak Portuguese at home when one of my brothers comes to visit me or if I have friends that come over. My kids, and they hold me accountable for that; they want to know why I didn't teach them the language. But circumstances did not allow for it.

As a banker I think you are in a good position to observe this. Recent news reports seem to argue that because of the weakening dollar and due to improving economic conditions at home, some Brazilians are packing up their bags and are returning to Brazil. Have you noticed this?
In Lowell, I did a study with the help of Linda [Silka] and the Center [for Family, Work and Community]. We estimated that there were about 15,000 Portuguese speakers. We did not want to come up with the actual Brazilian numbers, but better than half were Brazilians. The Brazilian population in Lowell three to four years ago had gone up to about 12,000 or more. The estimation now is about 7,000. And this past December one travel agency alone sold about seven hundred tickets one-way to Brazil. The estimation is that about 1,500 people have left and they continue to go back.

What is causing this decline?
The Brazilian economy has rebounded and there are some jobs being created. People, with the dollar being weak in Brazil, it's just getting more and more difficult to send money home because it's not worth as much. And to complicate matters, the immigration laws. Many Brazilians were hoping there would be some changes by now, but it's very difficult. More and more people are being stopped for traffic violations. You cannot get licenses. Jobs are becoming scarce. So they are looking to go back to Brazil, or they move to a different area of the country such as Florida, where there's a larger community there and they are able to get driver's licenses and

things like that. So, that's why there's this shift. Framingham is the biggest city that's being hit right now. But there has been an impact in Lowell where some of the businesses have a little bit of a concern. If you go to the Rios restaurant, for example, you would see six months ago, a year ago, they didn't have any people who spoke English. But now they have English speakers there because they are trying to make the conversion to attract other nationalities to maintain their earnings.

So it's hard for Brazilian businesses to keep up with the loss of population?
If they are catering exclusively to the Brazilians, yes.

Do you still go to St. Anthony's church?
Yes, that's my church.

Is it still primarily a Portuguese church?
Yes, there are some Brazilians who go there. But the majority of the Brazilians go to another church in the South Lowell area —the Holy Family Church. It's a church that came up in St. Mary's/Sacred Heart church merger. That's when they wanted to merge all the churches and we fought it. So, the majority of the Brazilians go to that new church, but some of them come to the Portuguese church.

I read somewhere that Pentecostalism is on the rise in Latin America, is that also the case with the Brazilians here in Lowell?
No, I think you have other denominations of the Christian faith. You have the Assembly of God Church that has a good following. You have a Seventh Day Adventist in Lowell. And you have Baptists churches. They all vary a little bit. Right down the street from the bank now is the Four Square Gospel church. It's a Brazilian church. But I never heard much about it. But there are quite a few churches in the area catering to the Brazilians.

Is there any interaction between the churches?
I have spoken to several of the pastors and I always blast them because I think if they put aside their differences and put the community first we would all be better off. There are many issues in the Brazilian community. Domestic violence… There are all kinds of social issues out there that have not been addressed because the leadership has not come together to address them. There's a movement now where some of the pastors are getting together. Hopefully they will get their act together

and come up with a way they can still protect their flock, but do something for the common good.

Have you ever had relatives come to visit you?
Yes, I have had some cousins and uncles eho came to visit. I had a brother who moved back to Brazil who's getting here tomorrow.

How long do folks stay when they come to visit?
Well, in his case, he's going to stay about six weeks, eight weeks. The others they stay a month, a month and a half.

Do you take them to any place in particular when they come to visit?
Well, Boston is a big deal. It's known in Brazil, so you want to visit some sites in Boston. Lowell? Not so much. There's really no attraction here in Lowell that people really want to go to, although I did find out that in the eighteen hundreds the then Brazilian Emperor came to Lowell to look at the mills. But there's really no connection for them.

Are you involved with some of the Portuguese festivals?
It depends. I grew up with the Portuguese festivals. My wife and I used to go to the Holy Ghost every time there was a festival. I can't say I've gone for the last five years because life changes, my kids are older; they have their own interests.

Do you still think it's important, or does is not play a central role any longer?
I think it does play a central role for the Portuguese community as a whole and I think that's what's keeping the Portuguese community together right now. One of the things I helped start and we backed off a little bit, we started a Portuguese networking group and five or six of us older people got together, invited the young people and said, now it's your thing, do what you want with it, and they are putting events together.

One of the things that is keeping the church going is the festivals. Without the festivals there would be no money to run the church.

Do Brazilians come to these festivals too or are they solely Portuguese?
The Brazilians do go to the festivals and they enjoy them, and the Brazilians have put a couple of their own festivals together too.

Obviously you don't vote in the city of Lowell anymore because you live in Tyngsboro but who do you think has the political power in Lowell?

As an ethnic group it's still the Irish. I feel that eventually when the other groups get their act together they may be able to have the power. Right now the power is concentrated in the old traditional families and so forth. But I think eventually the ethnic groups that are now the majority in Lowell, will realize that things will get accomplished the way they want to see it if they have the power. What's working against that? Power is not associated with good things and may have caused deaths in families and so forth. Not to the extent of the Cambodian genocide necessarily, but immigrants often see power as something they should not pursue. So that leaves a vacuum of power.

Would you like to see newer immigrants on the city council?

I think everybody should have a voice and it would be nice if the city council were representative of the community it serves or represents. I think that it will be a long time before that happens. Because the political system in Lowell and the form of government we have concentrates power. If you look at the last ten elections in Lowell, you may find that certain sections of the city did not get represented and those sections are where the majority of low income and immigrant groups are. So I think there would be resistance to change the at-large type of voting system that is used in Lowell, but there might be a way to maintain the at-large system, with a selected representation of certain areas. You might be able to reserve a certain number of seats for the Acre or Back Central or whatever so they have a representation. But that does not guarantee you that you're going to have someone from a certain ethnic group running for that seat either. The question here really is: Do you want to force something or should it happen naturally?

Have you personally experienced tensions between different ethnic groups in Lowell?

I think I have seen only part of it. Brazilian and Portuguese, I have lived some of the tensions. I have seen some tensions among different Hispanic community members because of where they are from. I went to a few parties and the Puerto Ricans would be upset because they would play cumbia all night, which is Columbian music, and not Puerto Rican salsa or meringue. Columbians would be upset the next dance because there was merengue and no cumbia, and they would leave and not go to the next party.

I don't think that any of the immigrant groups that come from different regions, for example the Africans, they're not yet a cohesive unit. They come from different parts and if they could just say: "We are Africans and we will squabble among ourselves when we are by ourselves, but to the outside world we are united." Or "We are Hispanics, and to the outside world we're going to be united," it doesn't matter if I come from Santo Domingo, Puerto Rico, or Columbia. We will squabble among ourselves when we're among our family here. But they have not learned how to do that. Even among the Brazilians there is mistrust because Brazil is a vast country and people from the southern part of Brazil may not get along with people from the northern part.

The Portuguese have two soccer clubs, the blue and red, and they don't seem to be able to coexist in a peaceful and productive manner. I say, keep the differences on the soccer field, but they bring them outside. From island to island there is a difference. So if they could just forget those regional things and just think I'm Portuguese, or I'm Brazilian, or African and we should be talking and working together. You would see a lot of nice things happening in these ethnic communities as opposed to the bickering, which weakens their position and therefore they cannot put on a united front to achieve what they really want.

Have you personally experienced discrimination because you are Brazilian?
I am not so sure the discrimination was because I'm Brazilian, but because I'm a foreigner. Most people, because of my accent, they can't distinguish if I'm Spanish or Brazilian or what. So I'm a foreigner. To that extent, over the last thirty-seven years, I have worked in a factory where the boss did not like foreigners. I was dipping circuit boards into acid and he gave me gloves that he put holes in. My hands were burning and I couldn't figure out what it was and he kept yelling at me because I wasn't working and stuff like that. My English at the time was not very good. I told you before about the fast food place.

Growing up the rivalry between Brazilian and Portuguese... I was with my wife at the Holy Ghost, and I was asked by the president to leave the dance floor and leave the premises because I was Brazilian and did not belong there, so that happened. Today I'm good friends with the person. At that time, trying to get married in the Portuguese church, my wife's grandmother had to intercede with the priest because the priest was not going to marry me because I was Brazilian.

As Chairman of the Board of the Salvation Army, because of my position there, one of my Board members offered the services of her daughter to give me speech therapy so I could get rid of this awful accent. Those types of things do happen and they have happened to me. I always took it with a smile. I just have to keep proving myself.

Do you feel like a Brazilian, Brazilian-American, American?
I am an American and proud to be an American. When I became a citizen, I did not become a citizen because this country had a lot to give me. I felt at that time that I needed to become a citizen because I had so much to give to the country. That's what I tried to do. But you can't forget who you are, because then all the qualities that made you go away. I am Brazilian. I got my foundation; I got everything that I believe in when I was in Brazil. I remember being ten, eleven years old and I was fascinated by the Kennedys and cried when John Kennedy got assassinated.

So when I came here, I at first, for the first three or four years, I hated this country. I wanted to go back. I was taken out of my country and brought to a foreign land with a different language, different customs, very cold, leaving my friends, and everything that I knew. I was not a very happy camper.

What changed my mind? God works in different ways I guess. In 1975 I had this cerebral aneurism and ended up in Boston. I had this surgery to correct the vein that was ready to burst. I realized then that if I was not in this country, I would be dead. If I were not in Boston.... I was at a hospital here in Lowell, which is no longer there, St. Josephs Hospital. I was blind at the time. One of the nurses [at St. Joseph's] told me to tell my family to get me to Boston because I was there to have surgery and they were going to kill me because they didn't know what they were doing. So at that point, I stopped to thank god. I had a nice conversation with him the night before my surgery and I came out of it with no defects at all. I came out better than when I went into the surgery.

So one of the things that I promised I would do is that I would take a look at this country with different eyes. And it was then that I decided to go back to school. I left the pizza place. Twenty years later from the day I started working there I bought the building and the business! That's when I started my banking career. Ever since then I decided to give back. So if you look at my resume, I probably have seventy five to a hundred organizations for which I have volunteered in different capacities, as a volunteer, as a board member, as Chair, you name it. When I was with the Coalition for a Better Acre I went in with all my heart and was able to, in my opinion, do a very good job in doing things that needed to be done while not selling my soul. We needed to work with the city and we did that. As a result there was an Acre plan that was a $70 million investment for the neighborhood. That made life much better for everybody. I'm very proud of that. The university used the communities as laboratories and I kept on hitting on the same point. "You need to give back." I was able to get the attention of then Chancellor William Hogan.

You said you are finishing up a degree?
Yes, in Community Economic Development at Southern New Hampshire University. It's a Master of Science degree. Throughout my life, even though I came to UMass Lowell, I never got my Bachelor's degree because the bill from the surgery I told you about was quite large. I had to pay that. Then I got married and bought a house and then I started my banking career. It never stopped me. I'm a vice-president of the bank. But I always said to myself that someday I'm going to go back and get a degree.

This program accepted me, based on my experience… But, will I go for a doctorate? Well, one day at a time. I've got to get my Master's Degree first and I'll finish in May. The best thing to come out of it is that I'm not going to just have a degree. I'm going to do something with it.

How do you think Lowell has changed since you got here?
It's been a very nice transformation. When I first got here, Lowell was really going downhill fast. Businesses were leaving. The last of the factories were going south. A lot of the businesses downtown were closing their doors. The downtown was starting to get boarded up… I remember crime was an issue. Then they started to talk about the National Park. Wang was building its headquarters downtown where Middlesex Community College is now. By the late 1970s there was hope for Lowell, and in the early 1980s you kind of saw everything coming together.

I remember back then reading a report that Lowell would become a university-city. It has not come to fruition yet. But I think everything is in place for it to happen. So, Lowell has turned around. I think that's why I bought the pizza place, university-city right downtown! I'll have a pizza place, and I'm still waiting for the university-city. But I think it will become a reality in the not too distant future.

I think they have done a nice job with Lowell. I think the only area where I might disagree with the policy makers and the power brokers is that they want to maintain the momentum by excluding low-income people from their agenda and I believe that that's wrong. It's wrong morally and it's wrong as part of their overall strategy. If Lowell is to become a destination city as they want it to be, or if it's going to become a university city, it doesn't matter which one it is, Lowell has to rely on the service industry, and the service industry is not one that is known for paying top dollars. So if you don't have affordable housing, where are you going to get your workers to provide the services? Are you going to use Lawrence? [A nearby former mill city with a similar history to Lowell, which has not developed as much as Lowell.]

Lawrence one of these days is going to get its act together. You're not going to get them [workers] from neighboring communities like Chelmsford or Dracut or Tewksbury or Tyngsboro. If we don't put something in place that allows for people from all walks of life to have a stake in Lowell, to make a contribution, I think we are missing the boat. So every chance I have, no matter what it is, I talk about affordable housing. Economic development can't happen without affordable housing. If I want to bring my factory and a hundred jobs to Lowell, where are my employees going to live?

What dreams do you have for your future, for your family's future, for the city's future?
I would like to see Lowell continue to emerge as a great city in which to work, live and play. I would like to see Lowell continue to create a more educational environment and the infrastructure that you need to make Lowell a vibrant city with options. For my family, I hope that my kids continue to pursue their education that they end up having some career where they have options and are happy with what they are doing. As far as my dream… My dream is to be able to call my own shots, and that's why I went back to get my diploma. I think with the diploma, I will be able to call my own shots. Very specifically I found out when I was executive director of the Coalition for a Better Acre that I have a passion in life. That passion is helping people. I try to do that at the bank. But I have to remember that the bank has shareholders and that's who pays my salary and that's who I have to satisfy. As much as the bank allows me to be part of the community, and volunteer my time, I feel that there is a lot more I could do, if I put my time and effort and talents to it. I could be making things easier for people.

So, I see myself in the not too distant future, maybe sooner than anybody would expect to be doing something in community economic development. Also I do have a business that I want to make sure is as vibrant as possible because that's my retirement fund. I want to continue to get along with my wife. We've been married 27 years. We went together for ten, so we've been together for 37 years. I want to keep that healthy and enjoy it.

Thank you so much for talking to us.

CHAPTER NINE

Muriel Parseghian

Muriel Parseghian, an Armenian American, came to the United States with her family in the 1960s. Muriel is an active member of the Armenian community. Christoph Strobel interviewed her on December 12, 2007.

> As a child, the U.S. was Hollywood, whatever I saw in the movies. We were big movie fans. I thought we were going to come and see that here. That really was the expectation. As a child, I could hear people talking and say, "Dollars grow on trees there." As a child you think that's true. That was the expectation.

I'd like to talk about the migration history of your family.
My particular family?

Why did they decide to come to the United States, where did you come from?
We came in 1963 from France. But in order for me to tell you how we ended up in Lowell in 1963 I have to go back almost seventy years. At the turn of the century, my extended family, at the time obviously my parents were not married, were living in what was called Anatolia and Asia Minor.

This was before the First World War, in the Ottoman Empire. There was what was called the "Milliett System." In the Ottoman Empire each ethnic group was under a different jurisdiction. For the Armenians it was the patriarchy – the religious patriarchy. At the turn of the century, when the pogroms began against the Armenians, which eventually culminated in the 1915 genocide, both sides of my family started to migrate out of their ancestral homes.

My parents come from two different areas of what we call western Armenia, or eastern Turkey. My father was born during the genocide in 1917. They took a different route than my mother's family. My father's family went from the town of Kutahya, which still exists today, and migrated to Istanbul. They eventually took a boat as refugees to Piraeus, Greece and they stayed there for quite a few years. He lost three of his siblings there and my uncle was born there. From there they went, as refugees again by boat, to Marseille.

My mother's family, my mother was a post-genocide baby, went the southern route into Syria through the Del Zor desert to the town of Aleppo, the second-largest city in Syria. There, in refugee camps, my grandparents met each other again. My grandmother was pregnant with my mother when they arrived in Marseille. I believe from Aleppo her family went down to Beirut and then by boat to France. But my parents lived in different refugee camps. So, my father was brought up in one refugee camp, my mother in another. I think there were half a dozen or so Armenian refugee camps in Marseille in the late 1920s–early 1930s.

My father became a French citizen by joining its army. Later, he met my mother and married her. We were in France for the first few years of my life. While my mother was living in France, her great-uncle had migrated to the United States. He ended up in Binghamton, New York, where there was a substantial Armenian community. There were factories there, Johnson & Murphy, I think, they made shoes. Anyways, little by little he brought our family over. First my uncle, my mother's brother, then he brought my cousins, then my aunt. So when it came time for us to come, he signed the paperwork and we were going to go to Binghamton, but one of my cousins met an Armenian woman from Lowell. They were moving to Lowell and we came to Lowell.

So your great-uncle was really the pull factor, because France, as far as I know, has a pretty sizeable Armenian community.
Yes, Marseille had 80,000 Armenians at the time we left, in a city of 600,000. Most of the people who came to the United States, even those who did not stay, came through Marseille. The French government at the end of the Ottoman Empire, at the end of World War I, was still involved with Syria and Lebanon, and that's where a lot of Armenians were so they brought them to Marseille. We ended up in Lowell. We could've ended up any place. The reason my cousin married a girl from Lowell was because there was a substantial Armenian community in Lowell.

Was there still a strong Armenian community here when you got to Lowell?
Yes. There were a lot of Armenians living in the city. There was the Armenian Church on Lawrence Street, which now I believe is a Spanish Pentecostal Church, but don't hold me to it. Although there was an Armenian church in Lowell, at the time we did not have a community center. There was a split in the Armenian Church—a political split. The community that did not go to the church on Lawrence Street had no place to gather. So in 1964 we bought the building on Liberty Street and that became our community center. I think the Lawrence Street church moved to Chelmsford. I want to say in the 1970s. They bought a piece of property there.

Are they still active there?
They're still there. Most Armenians in greater Lowell go to the church in Chelmsford or to the church in North Andover.

What were your expectations when you came from France to America, did you have certain preconceptions?
As a child, the U.S. was Hollywood, whatever I saw in the movies. We were big movie fans. I thought we were going to come and see that here. That really was the expectation. As a child, I could hear people talking and say, "Dollars grow on trees there." As a child you think that's true. That was the expectation.

How did you come over?
By boat. We took the train from Marseille to Paris and we stayed there for a couple of days. Then we took a train from Paris to The Hague. Then we took the boat. We stopped in London but didn't get off and we ended up in New York City. The name of the boat was the USS United States. And then from New York my cousin, the one who was getting married to the woman from Lowell, came to pick us up. Funny thing we remember distinctly because he came with his future father-in-law who had a Cadillac. In those days a Cadillac had wings, so when we saw them we said: "We came to America."

Did your family have an expectation of staying in Lowell for a limited amount of time?
We did not have any expectations to go anywhere else. My mother wanted to be reunited with her family. Actually, the only expectation was that we knew my parents were going to be able to get jobs, steady jobs, and economically we were going to do better.

Have you become a citizen?

We became citizens really quickly, five years into it. The moment we could, we became citizens.

Did your folks bring relatives to the U.S.?

My grandma, my paternal grandmother, did come. She came as a tourist and at the time Bradford Morse was our Congressperson and at Lowell city hall there was a man named Michael Ansara. He was in charge of immigrants. When it came time for my grandmother to leave, Ansara asked us, "Do you want her to stay?" Of course we did. So he placed a call to Bradford Morse and at the time Congress passed a law just for her to stay. She stayed and she died here. We did bring her, but no one else.

You mentioned how the Armenian community has changed and is maybe even disappearing. At least this is somewhat of a feeling I had when I came to visit you at the Center. It was a theme that a lot of people brought up. You've lived in Lowell since the 1960s?

Since 1963. I went away to college, and I went to school in Lebanon. I left Lowell for a total of maybe ten years on and off.

Do you consider yourself as being a part of a neighborhood today?

Not from the Armenian sense, no.

Did you have that feeling in the 1960s?

I saw Lowell as a neighborhood with a very active Armenian community. There was the support that a community provides and there was a social aspect. Where we lived on Fort Hill Avenue we had four Armenian neighbors on that one block, us and four other families. I did not consider this to be an Armenian section. We had Armenian neighbors. But I did consider Lowell to be an Armenian city at the time.

Were there more Armenian businesses at the time? How do you do your shopping today compared to the 1960s? Was there an Armenian store you could go to, Armenian businesses, Armenian lawyers, etc.?

Right, there was an Armenian tailor. You would go to him. There were Armenian hairdressers. Everybody's related too, by marriage, or by acquaintance, and you felt as if you knew these people. Obviously, there are some Armenian merchants and commerce people, but I don't seek them out. I mean, I don't need to seek them out the way the previous generation did.

Can you elaborate on that?

When my father went to get his driver's license, he saw that there were two Armenians working. He sought out one of the Armenians. Not that the guy was going to give him a break, but he was certainly going to feel like, this guy is going to understand me, he is not going to have a difficult time understanding my language or what I'm saying. You go to an Armenian barber, or go to the Armenian locksmith, whoever had an Armenian business you would solicit them. Not only to support them financially but I think it gave my parents' generation a certain level of confidence.

They walked in and it was easy to do business with them, there was no trying to explain things. Even when you went to Espresso Pizza, there was one Armenian guy working there, so my father would always go to him to order the pizza. Today, I do not need to do that. I'm very comfortable going into any store. That's the difference.

Do you think that it was a need for community for them as well?

They had a community socially, obviously, because all Armenians, we all know each other. We get together for different events. I don't know so much if they went there because they felt the need to re-establish what they had in France, of living in an Armenian ghetto. I really think for my parents, anyways, it was the fact that it was very easy, the guy knew Armenian words or he understood them and if they asked for something unusual, the guy understood. I think it was more a level of comfort. Being an immigrant, you just felt comfortable talking to somebody who understood you.

That makes sense. I think you see that playing out in the newer communities as well. Obviously the Armenian center plays an important role. But you do have non-Armenian friends?

Right, right. Like most immigrants I think we straddle two worlds. I have my Armenian world and then I have my non-Armenian world. There are some friends who are able to function in both circles. For the greater majority, the two of them are almost parallel.

I'd like to flesh out a little more the comparison between your life in Marseille and your life in Lowell. You refer to Marseille as the "Armenian ghetto."

It was an Armenian ghetto. At first, the Armenians were in refugee camps. It was literally camps. Towards the end of the 1930s, before Second World War broke out, there was the beginning of movement from the camps into neighborhoods. Basically, what people did was go from shacks to homes. The only non-Armenians I came across were my teacher, the doctor, the mailman, and the garbage collector. The school I went to was about 40 percent Armenian and the classmates I was friends with, they were all Armenian. So, we lived in a totally Armenian world.

When we came here, like I said, we had neighbors on the block who were Armenian but there were no children. The immediate friends I had on the block were not Armenian. That was really my first exposure to non-Armenian people. The biggest thing was: "Oh this is what people eat. They eat different things than us." All these things that you get exposed to that you were never exposed to before.

In terms of language, in France, did you speak Armenian a lot?
Right, everybody spoke Armenian because the elderly, my grandparents' generation, they never learned to speak French. Some of them spoke Turkish. My grandparents were Turkish speaking. Everybody spoke Armenian.

When you came to Lowell did you speak Armenian with your family?
We spoke Armenian and French because my sisters and I had obviously gone to school so we were comfortable speaking French amongst each other. But you know, with my aunt and others, certainly with the Armenian community we spoke Armenian.

Do you have a sense that these languages are still passed on to the next generation?
It's passed on in a limited way. What happened with the Armenian community, in the 1970s we got a new wave of immigrants from the Middle East. Most of them came from Lebanon and of course from Iran. The Iranian Armenians speak the eastern dialect, which is the same dialect that is spoken in Armenia today. We speak the western dialect, the Syrians and the Lebanese.

In the 1970s, there was a resurgence of the language being spoken. But it is dying out now. Very few people force their children to speak Armenian. Before, you were forced to. Your parents wouldn't talk to you unless you answered back in Armenian. There are some Armenian schools now. There are two Armenian schools in greater Boston.

One of the scholarly perceptions about the Middle East and about the people from that region is the strength of the family. Do you think that is the case in the Armenian community?
Yes, that's true. Your family is extremely important. They're in your life. It's not

unusual for an aunt to give the nephew advice that he does not even seek. You know, "you should do this, you should do that," that's it. It is changing obviously, but yes Armenians are very family-oriented.

How do families stay together? I mean, obviously there used to be more of a community around, do you feel that becomes a challenge for families?

Yes, it does. What happened is that people left because of jobs, or they left because they married another Armenian. What has happened to our community, I don't know if you picked up on that when you came to visit our community center, many of those who stayed here married non-Armenians. They sort of re-strengthened the community. The Armenians who married Armenians went to large Armenian communities. Many who are active in our community are married to non-Armenians.

So they moved to places like Watertown?

Watertown or even California. A lot of people from Lowell moved to California

Was that a 1980s development or is it more recent?

The ones who came from the Middle East and who came to Lowell only stayed here for 5,6,7,8 years and eventually moved to California because they had relatives there or because California resembles much more the Middle Eastern lifestyle. And then, in the 1980s, in the 1990s, as people, my contemporaries and those younger than me, started thinking about getting married there was, if you met somebody, you'd say: "Ah, he lives in California." People would stay committed to the relationship and move. The economy and the situation here is not that appealing to most people so they went to where their spouses were.

Particularly to the Los Angeles area, right?

Yes.

Do you feel that your life is different from that of your parents? How has your life changed from that of your parents? You already said that you don't need the kind of safety net that your parents needed.

One thing I can say is that my parents came here for economic opportunities. My sisters and I achieved that. They may not have achieved it to the level we did because they came here late or whatever but certainly they gave my sisters and me the opportunity to do that. That has made a big difference. I can say that for all

Armenians who came. Within one generation people had bought property, they were in business, they were educated. That's the American dream and for the most part Armenians achieved it. I can say Armenians achieved the American dream, that's for sure.

Do you consider yourself an American at this point or an Armenian-American?
When I'm in this country, I'm an Armenian-American. I'm the most American when I'm with other Armenians from all over the world. As you know, I belong to a few organizations and when we have international meetings Armenians come from all over the world, that's when I really feel that I'm an American.

You say that some people made the choice to move to larger Armenian communities to pass on the cultural heritage and language to their children. Within Lowell do you feel that there is an effort to teach the history, obviously the genocide is very central.
Armenians are a politicized people. So there is an effort to pass things on to the next generation. It's like a duty you feel. It's in our psyche. You have to do that. Even the Armenian that's only one-fourth Armenian feels compelled to do that. You take great pride in who you are! You have to pass it on to your children.

I want to make another giant leap over to the issue of economics. You already mentioned that your economic situation as compared to your parents has really improved. I don't know whether that's part of the generational sacrifice that your parents made. I know that in a lot of immigrant communities folks still support a family network back home, was that the case with your family in France?
In America you had things that you didn't have in other parts of the world. You have gadgets, you have toys. Even to this day we send things back to France. Not because they cannot afford it but because of the abundance of it here and the quality. It's relatively cheap. But it's not that we're supporting them. We give them luxury items that otherwise they would not get.

I know when we were in France and something would come from America, it was a big deal. Everybody wants something from America, like my 14 year-old cousin wanted a Denver Broncos [football] shirt…. They love American things. I remember living in France, we loved American things. There's something about American products. They're just appealing. The same thing when people go to Armenia. They just bring a lot of stuff with them. There's just something appealing about it.

I remember, but maybe I'm confusing this now with someone else I talked to during the night, but your family is really from what is now eastern Turkey? Do I remember that correctly?

My family is from central Turkey. They migrated from the eastern part of Turkey, maybe five to ten centuries ago. I don't know when exactly they moved.

The reason why I'm asking this question is because I remember that you said at some point that when you go to what is Armenia today, it doesn't feel like home to you.

Correct, it's not. That was a very small portion of Armenia. It is a different culture that was influenced by the Russians and Iran, while the Greeks and the Turks influenced us. It is different. Even our grammar is different because of the influences of other cultures.

Do you still feel, however, that there is a tie with the state of Armenia? Is there an effort with you or people you know within the Armenian community to support the Armenian state?

Yes, one thing people do, we support charities there, orphanages, hospitals. We send money to relatives. Of course, we travel there to get the economy going. It's almost understood that you have to make at least one pilgrimage there. Armenian-Americans don't say, 'did you go to Armenia?' They say 'when did you go to Armenia?' It's become part of the culture. Some people go every year. There are people who buy houses there. They go there and instead of buying a house in Florida they buy it there. There is a very strong attachment to go there. You have to go there. How long it's going to last? I don't know.

People will go because it's a beautiful country and visit historic things. I don't know how long the emotional and economic support will last. Frankly, being an old Soviet Union country, it still has a lot of inequality, which is unpleasant. So, there are some frustrations in that respect.

How would you describe your life in Lowell now? Do you feel like your life is economically comfortable here? Do you feel like you're solidly middle-class? Your employment is good?

I feel like I'm middle-class. I've got a good job. I had the opportunity to go to school. I would say I'm middle-class. I own my house. Well, the bank owns it, but you know. Like I said, I think I've reached the goals of my parents, what they thought would happen by moving here.

I've become much more assimilated. I lived in France and I lived in Lebanon and there are huge Armenian communities in both places and you never felt you were part of France or Lebanon. Lebanon is a little bit more complicated but you were an Armenian in Lebanon. In France, you were an Armenian too. It has changed now, because a lot of Armenians have given up being Armenian. They've become French. Here, I feel as if I can be Armenian and there's no issue. I'm fine.

What were you doing in Lebanon?
I went to school there in 1983-1984. It was an Armenian school. There was supposed to be peace then, but it didn't happen. There was a huge Armenian community in Lebanon, huge.

Did they leave with the civil war?
They started to leave in the 1950s. People don't know that in the 1950s there was civil unrest in Lebanon; so they started leaving. They moved everywhere. They moved to the United States, some to France. Some moved to Dubai, Kuwait, you know. But most people came to Los Angeles.

Social networks and religion is another theme we're interested in, the kind of religious services you attend, the center and your involvement there, and so on.
The Armenian Church is a national church so it's not only a Christian church. We pride ourselves on being the first nation to adopt Christianity. The church really ran the nation. I mentioned that there was a political split. That created some issues, particularly in this country, but the church is very important. Not only for religious reasons, but because it's your national church and it's your community. In my grandparent's generation they would go to church a lot. My parent's generation, little by little, got away from it.

What has happened to the Armenian Church is that when people have children, young children, they'll come to the church until the children are fourteen or fifteen and don't want to go anymore. Then they stop coming regularly. They'll come on holidays. They usually come at Easter because the forty days of Lent is a big thing in our church. They come to the Armenian Christmas. Then they'll come back again when they're older. So, if you go to our church you see there are parents with young children and elderly people. Those whose children are in college are not around. They used to be around but they're not around anymore.

Some of the churches in the U.S. are struggling a little bit because people moved out into the suburbs and they don't want to drive to the city to go to the Armenian churches. The number one reason I go to church is funerals and memorial services. That is my particular thing. There are other Armenians who go for different things. I'll go a few other times. People do get married and christened. That's probably how the churches survive – funerals, marriages, and christenings.

Growing up I belonged to the Armenian Youth Federation. We had a chapter in Lowell. That was my social network. We would meet on weekends and then we would go out. I started when I was ten until about thirty. And of course you would go away. You go to other communities where there were Armenians and we would get together. To this day those people are still my friends. That's how we basically stick together, through these organizations, because otherwise you don't see each other. Everybody just has too much of a busy lifestyle to see each other. But these things force you. Like that dinner you came to at the Armenian Center. It forces everybody to come together and so if you do that four or five times a year; it keeps the community together.

Do you have a favorite holiday, like Lent or Christmas?
I like everything from Armenian Christmas to the Lent celebration. I like that because we see each other a lot. Even for the planning you get to see people who you usually don't see. In the summers we participate in the folk festival. That really helps to bring our community together.

What's the Armenian community's involvement with the folk festival?
We have a food booth. We also used to be part of the regatta festival before the folk festival. We used to even belong to the International Institute. They used to have events. We've always been part of some kind of event here. When there used to be a JFK Plaza Memorial Day Weekend, before the Folk Festival came to Lowell, we used to do that. We've been there forever. We were at JFK Plaza next to the beer booth. Last year we took a break because we were just a little bit overwhelmed, but this year we came back.

A lot of members of the Armenian community have moved away or moved to the suburbs. You said that Lowell used to be an Armenian town. Do you still feel that way? As an ethnic group are the Armenians involved in Lowell politics?
There are a lot of Armenians involved. But it feels as if their involvement has little

to do with them being Armenian. I mean nobody brings the Armenian banner to these things. I don't feel as if the presence of Armenians in Lowell reflects the presence of a strong Armenian community.

Do you make political decisions or do you support people because they're Armenian or have you moved beyond that?
Me personally? I've moved beyond that.

Do you think there are people still within the Armenian community who only support Armenians?
Yes, of course, the older people. I'm fifty-five, but people older than me. Every time they see the 'ian' they will support that person. Yes, there are some people like that.

Do you find that certain ethnic groups hold a disproportionate amount of power in Lowell?
Of course. The only way Armenians got into politics was by not having the Armenian banner any more. I don't think Alan Kazanjian's [a city council in Lowell at the time of the interview] father, for sure not his grandfather, could have run. People see him as Armenian, but they don't see him as a foreigner. I think his father and grandfather would've been looked upon differently. I've been in Lowell since 1963 and it's the same power base. It's very difficult for newcomers.

Would you like to see more of the recent immigrants being involved?
Of course. But the oligarchy has not allowed anybody else to come in. It's funny, they talk about Irish-Americans and French-Canadians and Greeks, but that's it.

Have you personally experienced tensions between different ethnic groups in Lowell in your lifetime? Growing up, did you feel sometimes that you were discriminated against as an Armenian?
Because I'm a little brown-skinned, and people don't know what I am, they made assumptions that I was Hispanic and they would say nasty things. There was that part. Nobody knew what Armenian was. So they ask, "what are you?" Because I spoke with an accent and my skin was a little browner I was often mistook. That kind of discrimination…. I was made to feel at times like the outsider.

Do you feel at times that you are typecast as a Middle Easterner or is that not an issue?
Good point. With 9/11 that again became an issue. People would say, "Are you Palestinian?" That kind of thing. "Aren't you from Pakistan? No, I'm Armenian."

Then you have to give them a history and geography lesson. That was always an issue up to the 1960s and 1970s, even some of the 1980s.

I'll give you a perfect example. During the Iranian crisis my social circle of Armenian friends, those who would go out, there used to be a Howard Johnson, which became a Ground Round and it was open almost twenty-four hours. So we would always go at 11:30PM or midnight, to get something to eat. Once, we walked in as a group and somebody yells out, "Don't feed those f***ing Iranians." You know… that kind of thing. And then my cousin who was playing soccer, he has very dark skin, somebody kicked him and somebody yelled out: "Don't worry, he's only Iranian."

Do you feel there are tensions within the Armenian community? Maybe regional differences, or do you feel that people seem to, I don't want to call it unified, but beyond the usual squabbles that occur among people…

I think what has happened, because most Armenians are doing quite well economically, everybody seems to be more comfortable with where they are personally. The problem is that everybody wants his or her own fiefdom. There's a struggle within the Armenian community among different groups to achieve the same thing. There will be five, ten groups trying to build the same thing. I'm just giving you an example, trying to build the same hospital, that kind of thing. That's the problem with the Armenian community.

Then, of course, politically how you feel about what is going on in Armenia and how much of a commitment you want to have to genocide recognition vis-à-vis the U.S. government. Some people say, "Oh, don't offend the Congress." Others say, "Hell with Congress." That's what today's reality is.

That's currently a pretty big issue, especially with the genocide issue. You obviously went to high school in Lowell. Did you go to the public school?
Yes, I went to Lowell public schools. I graduated in 1971.

And you went off to college?
To Northeastern University in Boston, right.

Did you find that there were good educational opportunities in Lowell when you were going to school?
I was very fortunate. When we came we didn't speak English. We started school at the Morey and then my aunt bought a house and we moved to Fort Hill Avenue and

we switched schools to Oakland, which is now the LeBlanc School. The teacher I had, I'll never forget his name. His name was Robert Timmons. He was a guy, fifth grade, and he couldn't have been kinder. There was a woman that would come in once a week to do remedial reading for the kids who couldn't read. I didn't even know what that was. She would teach me English.

Then sixth grade I had Mr. Quirbach. I never knew his first name. He would push me, push me, push me and maybe within the third month of the sixth grade, I had caught up. I think having those two guys was helpful. Then after that, at Moody again I was very fortunate to have great teachers. Mr. Sullivan the principal always pushed me. Then Lowell High was a madhouse. There were so many issues… Half of my teachers were fine, the other half, it was just a disaster there in that sense. I found that early on I had that help, the people just made me feel comfortable and the teachers I had, pushed you, "you can do it, you can do it."

By the time I got to Lowell High there were quite a few immigrants there from different countries. There was a kid from Jordan, there were Czechoslovakians. It's funny. There was a kid from Egypt. All the foreigners, I knew who they were. I don't know why. There was not a large group coming in, but there were immigrants.

Did you find that it gave you a support network?
I had my friends who I had originally met at the Oakland school. From Oakland we went to Moody together. I had a small circle. There were a lot of Armenians there and instantly we became friends.

I'd like to switch over to healthcare.
It's a good question, because when I think about it, we didn't have a doctor. We did not have a family doctor. I don't know why. We just…I can't remember.

What did your family do when you got sick?
You went to the hospital, or hoped you did not get sick. Healthcare was not on the radar screen. My father had a heart attack in 1970, when he was 53. He had his doctor because he had a number of heart attacks.

Were there any Armenian home medicines you were using?
For sure, especially when my grandparents were alive and lived with us. I remember they put cups, do you know this thing? If your back hurts there's these cups they'll put cotton on a fork and dip it in alcohol and burn the cotton. Then, put the cotton in

the cup and put the cup, like a suction cup, on your back. So, your whole back would be full of that and then they'll pop it. There were all kinds of things. I remember meat being put on all kinds of stuff. You had to have mint tea. I don't know if it works. My sisters and I still do it: 'I don't feel good. I'll have a cup of mint tea.' We grew the mint ourselves and dried it. There was a lot of that.

Do you still grow your own mint and make the tea?
One of my neighbors grows it. I get hers. There are a lot of Armenians who grow their own tea. It grows very easy. A lot of people grow it and dry it.

So this is something that you continue to do?
That tea portion, yeah, we still all do it. I don't think you can go into any Armenian household that doesn't have dried mint leaves.

Obviously Lowell has changed a lot since you came here. Do you have any dreams for the future, for the Armenian community, for your homeland, for your family, for yourself? Where would you like to see the story head?
You know, for the longest time Armenia was not independent, so we always talked about how one day we'll have an independent, united, free Armenia and we'll all go back. Well, they became free in 1993 and nobody went back. We go, we visit, because like I said earlier, I've become American, you know, whatever that is.

In Lowell, I really feel now that I'm a part of the community. Maybe it's because of my character, but it took a lot of time, but I feel that I'm part of the community. When I was in school I did not feel like that. I felt like a stranger. I didn't want to bring people to my house because we had different customs and they would not understand why my parents do things this way, that my parents don't speak English... Maybe because I'm mature, I'm an older person now, but I feel I'm part of Lowell.

Having said that, it doesn't mean that I'm part of the power base, not me personally, it's not that. I do feel I'm part of Lowell. My dreams for the Armenian community in Lowell is really to be able to sustain ourselves a little bit longer and, at least, to be able to have those who are a half or a quarter Armenian still carry on the traditions. I think it will happen. I really believe most human beings want to belong to a community. Armenians offer that. So, if your parent is a quarter Scottish or a quarter Irish, there's no community left, there's nothing, but [for] Armenians there is a structure, there's an instant community. That makes people, as human beings, feel much more fulfilled.

The dreams that I have for the homeland? I'd like it to be more politically stable, more progressive. Like I said earlier, it's corrupt. I'd like to see the other lands that belong to Armenia eventually unite with Armenia. Of course, I'd like to see the genocide recognized and Turkey accept it and give some reparations. That's what I would like to see.

If there's one thing, and this is the perfect universe question, but if there's one thing you could change about your experiences as an immigrant in Lowell, what would it be?
I would have forced my parents to speak English immediately. They would have had a better life. Read and write in English and become a little bit more assimilated. They had non-Armenian friends, but it was limited. I think, especially later on in life when they got old and sick, they would have had a better quality of life. The fact that they did not speak English well, they did not write it, they did not read it. I would have liked them to do that. To this day I don't understand why they didn't do it. I guess when you're a certain age you're too tired to learn, I don't know.

I think it's hard. I think you're right. This is the final question. If you were to ask a question about the experiences of immigrants in Lowell, what would it be?
That's a good question. I think one thing I don't understand about immigrants is why they're not more politicized, why their children aren't politicized. I can understand it on an intellectual level. But we have immigrants from a lot of different places in the world and this seems to be a common theme. I mean, you really, really have to work hard to politicize people and I don't know why that is.

I've really learned a lot. Thank you so much.

END NOTES

[1] Marc Rodriguez, ed., *Repositioning North American Migration History*, (Rochester, New York: University of Rochester Press, 2004), ix.

[2] Frederick W. Coburn, *History of Lowell and Its People* (New York City: Lewis Historical Publishing Company, 1920), 2; Paul F. McGouldrick, *New England Textiles in the Nineteenth Century: Profits and Investment*, Harvard Economic Studies, Vol. 131 (Cambridge: Harvard University Press, 1968), 13.

[3] Christoph Strobel, *Daily Life of the New Americans: Immigration since 1965* (Santa Barbara: Greenwood Press, 2010).

[4] See graph in Mitra Das, *Between Two Cultures: The Case of Cambodian Women in America* (New York: Peter Lang, 2007), 56.

[5] Hai Pho, "Lowell, Politics, and the Resettlement of Southeast Asian Refugees and Immigrants, 1975-2000," in *Southeast Asian Refugees and Immigrants in the Mill City: Changing Families, Communities, Institutions – Thirty Years Afterward*, eds., Tuyet-Lan Pho, Jeffrey N. Gerson, and Sylvia Cowan (Burlington, Vt.: University of Vermont Press, 2007), 15-16; Neeraj Kaushal, Cordelia Reimers, and David Reimers, "Immigrants and the Economy," in *The New Americans: A Guide to Immigration Since 1965* (Cambridge: Harvard University Press, 2007), 176-188.

[6] Hai Pho, "Lowell, Politics, and the Resettlement of Southeast Asian Refugees and Immigrants," 12.

[7] Tony Mai interviewed by Christoph Strobel, April 25, 2008, Ethnographic Study of Lowell, MA.

[8] Sylvia Cowan, Lao Refugees in Lowell: Reinterpreting the Past, Finding Meaning in the Present," in *Southeast Asian Refugees and Immigrants in the Mill City*, 135-137.

[9] Sucheng Chan, *Survivors: Cambodian Refugees in the United States* (Urbana: University of Illinois Press, 2004), 102-106.

[10] See for example Phala Chea interviewed by Christoph Strobel, January 15, 2008, Ethnographic Study of Lowell, MA; Sidney Liang interviewed by Christoph Strobel, January 17, 2008, Ethnographic Study of Lowell, MA.

[11] Eleanor E. Glaessel-Brown, "A Time of Transition: Colombian Textile Workers in Lowell in the 1970s," in *The Continuing Revolution: A History of Lowell, Massachusetts*, ed. Robert Weible (Lowell: Lowell Historical Society, 1991), 343-369.

[12] Anonymous 5 (Hispanic) interviewed by Christoph Strobel, February 5, 2008, Ethnographic Study of Lowell, MA.

[13] See for example K.N. Chaudhuri, *Asia before Europe: Economy and Civilisation of the Indian Ocean from the Rise of Islam to 1750* (Cambridge: Cambridge University Press,1985), 307-308.

[14] Raymond Brady Williams, *An Introduction to Swaminarayan Hinduism* (New York: Cambridge University Press, 2001), 209; Anonymous 1 (Indian) and Anonymous 2 (Indian) interviewed by Christoph Strobel, December 14, 2007, Ethnographic Study of Lowell, MA; Anonymous 4 (Indian) interviewed by Christoph Strobel, March 12, 2008, Ethnographic Study of Lowell, MA.

[15] Samkhann Khoeun interviewed by Susan Thomson and Christoph Strobel, January 8, 2008, Ethnographic Study of Lowell, MA.

[16] Samkhann Khoeun interviewed by Susan Thomson and Christoph Strobel, January 8, 2008, Ethnographic Study of Lowell, MA.

[17] See for example Alejandro Portes and Ruben Rumbaut, *Immigrant America*, Third Ed. (Berkeley: University of California Press, 2006), chapter 4; and Leakhena Nou, "Exploring the Psychosocial Adjustment of Khmer Refugees in Massachusetts from an Insider's Perspective," in *Southeast Asian Refugees and Immigrants in the Mill City*, 173-174.

[18] Ivan Light, "Disadvantaged Minorities in Self Employment," *International Journal of Comparative Sociology* 20 (March-June 1979), 31-45; Hillary Chabot, "'We Have to Sacrifice:' Immigrants struggling to develop small Businesses in Greater Lowell," *Lowell Sun*, March 12, 2006.

[19] See for example Samkhann Khoeun interviewed by Susan Thomson and Christoph Strobel, January 8, 2008, Ethnographic Study of Lowell, MA; Tony Mai interviewed by Christoph Strobel, April 25, 2008, Ethnographic Study of Lowell, MA; Anonymous 1 (Indian) and Anonymous 2 (Indian) interviewed by Christoph Strobel, December 14, 2007, Ethnographic Study of Lowell, MA; Bowa Tucker interviewed by Christoph Strobel, January 10, 2008, Ethnographic Study of Lowell, MA.

[20] Osvalda Rodrigues interviewed by Christoph Strobel, February 5, 2008, Ethnographic Study of Lowell, MA.

[21] Gordon Halm interviewed by Christoph Strobel, January 16, 2008, Ethnographic Study of Lowell, MA.

[22] Gloria Negri, "Cameroonian group praised for advancing race relations," *Boston Sunday Globe*, June 2, 2002.

[23] Tony Mai interviewed by Christoph Strobel, April 25, 2008, Ethnographic Study of Lowell, MA; Thong Phamduy interviewed by Christoph Strobel, April 30, 2008, Ethnographic Study of Lowell, MA; Bryan Tran interviewed by Christoph Strobel, Craig Thomas, and Yingchan Zhang, Mai 8, 2008, Ethnographic Study of Lowell, MA.

[24] Peter Occhiogrosso, *The Joy of Sects: A Spirited Guide to the World's Religious Traditions* (New York: Doubleday, 1994), 8.

[25] Robert Mills, "Local Indians look to native country amid news of horror," October 9, 2005, *Lowell Sun*; Robert Mills, "BAPS walk-a-thon raises funds for Hurricane Katrina survivors," October 10, 2005, *Lowell Sun*; Anonymous 1 (Indian) and Anonymous 2 (Indian) interviewed by Christoph Strobel, December 14, 2007, Ethnographic Study of Lowell, MA.

[26] Michael Lafleur, "'The Bigger your Fishing Net': Growing Lowell Church looking for New Home," *Lowell Sun*, January 23, 2007. See also Rita Ofori-Frimpong interviewed by Susan Thomson and Christoph Strobel, November 8, 2007, Ethnographic Study of Lowell; Gordon Halm interviewed by Christoph Strobel, January 16, 2008, Ethnographic Study of Lowell; Emile Tabea interviewed by Christoph Strobel, January 16, 2008, Ethnographic Study of Lowell.

[27] Jeffrey Gerson, "The Battle for Control of the Trairatanaram Cambodian Temple," in *Southeast Asian Refugees and Immigrants in the Mill City*, 153-172. See also Sidney Liang interviewed by Christoph Strobel, January 17, 2008, Ethnographic Study of Lowell; Sambath Bo interviewed by Christoph Strobel, April 15, 2008, Ethnographic Study of Lowell, MA.

[28] For quote, http://www.lowellwaterfestival.org/. Accessed February, 19, 2009.

[29] See also Strobel, 89.

[30] Wilson Wanene, "Puerto Rican pride rules in Lowell's Movable Feast," *Lowell Sun*, July 8, 2002.

[31] Dennis Shaughnessey, "Standing Tall," *Lowell Sun*, June 16, 2002.

[32] *The Angkor Dance Troupe* (Lowell, MA: Official Pamphlet of the Angkor Dance Troupe, 2003), 3-8.

[33] See for example the documentary *Monkey Dance*, by Julie Mallozzi (ITVS, NAATA, WGBH, 2005).

[34] Osvalda Rodrigues interviewed by Christoph Strobel, February 5, 2008, Ethnographic Study of Lowell, MA.

[35] David Turcotte and Linda Silka, "Reflections on the Concept of Social Capital" in *Southeast Asian Refugees and Immigrants in the Mill City*, 57-59.

[36] Rita Ofori-Frimpong interviewed by Susan Thomson with Christoph Strobel, November 8, 2007, Ethnographic Study of Lowell.

[37] Emile Tabea interviewed by Christoph Strobel, January 16, 2008, Ethnographic Study of Lowell.

[38] Ivette Nieves interviewed by Christoph Strobel and Yingchan Zhang, April 24, 2008, Ethnographic Study of Lowell, MA.

ABOUT THE COVER ARTISTS

Anabelle Souza is a senior at Lowell High School. In her own words Annablle says, "It's because of my experience at the Revolving Museum that I was able to expand my artistic ability and make a lot of friends who helped me become a better artist." After graduation in June 2011, Anabelle plans to pursue her BFA in illustration or painting.

Atena Vilorio is a senior at Lowell High School. Atena says, "Without the Museum I wouldn't know what to do. It has helped me get through so much. It's not just a place to learn about art and community, but has become my second home." Upon graduation in June 2011, Atena will attend Middlesex Community College.